THEY WERE HERE BEFORE US

THEY WERE HERE BEFORE US

Ran Barkai and Eyal Halfon

Translated from Hebrew by Eylon Levy

WATKINS
1893

They Were Here Before Us
Ran Barkai and Eyal Halfon

This edition first published in the UK and USA in 2024
by Watkins, an imprint of Watkins Media Limited
Unit 11, Shepperton House
89–93 Shepperton Road
London N1 3DF

enquiries@watkinspublishing.com

1 2 3 4 5 6 7 8 9 10

Designed and typeset by JCS Publishing Ltd

Printed and bound by CPI Group (UK) Ltd, Croydon, CR0 4YY

A CIP record for this book is available from the British Library

ISBN: 978-1-78678-831-3 (Paperback)
ISBN: 978-1-78678-832-0 (eBook)

www.watkinspublishing.com

MIX
Paper | Supporting
responsible forestry
FSC
www.fsc.org   FSC® C171272

CONTENTS

A VERY SHORT
INTRODUCTION

One of the first chapters in this book tells a story of a swan. A prehistoric swan. OK, not a whole swan, just its wing. In fact, not even its wing, just a piece of a wing, a bone fragment stripped of its feathers. This tiny discovery was made in the bowels of a cave inhabited by human beings 400,000 years ago. It took meticulous sifting, endless patience, tremendous experience, and academic imagination to understand that it once belonged to a swan with breathtaking plumage. In some sense, this swan's wing encapsulates the story that we are about to tell.

Because *someone* made the effort to haul this swan from a faraway place to this cave, and this someone had reasons for taking the trouble to do so and for picking a swan specifically, as opposed to a dove, or a sparrow, or a goose. This someone did not haul the swan all the way to the cave for a gourmet dinner. No, it was probably the swan's beautiful feathers, regal appearance, and ability to soar to the heavens that grabbed this cave-dweller's attention.

There are other far-flung places in the world, no less ancient, where similar discoveries have been made: remains of swans, vultures, or eagles. And this is all fascinating, not because of the birds themselves, but because of the people who interacted with them. *Our ancestors.* Those who lived here, roamed these lands, hunted, crafted tools, taught their children manners, made plans, and enjoyed watching the sun rise and set, and rise and set again.

Those who were here long before us.

This is not a book about archeological sites. We shall come across flint tools, bones, skulls, surprising structures, and layers of earth that we can date to different periods—but they are not the heart of the matter. This book is about *us*—human beings—and about our place in the world. About the amazing things we have done, where we came from, which other humans used to be here, why they are no longer with us, and how and why our lives have changed so much. It's also about where we went wrong. What did early humans do because they had no choice, or because they failed to gauge the consequences of their actions? What price are we all paying for this nowadays and will we continue to pay for it in the future?

Our journey began more than two million years ago in Africa, but the main stations on our tour are almost within walking distance of each other: from the Negev Desert in the south of modern-day Israel to the Golan Heights in the north of the country, in what used to be a major corridor between Africa and the rest of the world. These geographic stations are the gateways to a range of periods and topics in the history of humanity: migration, faith, the mastery of fire, technological innovation, relations with animals and our dependence on them, the importance of stones and minerals, conservatism versus the need for perpetual change, death and burial, and even the significance of human consciousness and its different states.

The stations may all be clustered in a narrow band of land, but each can also be considered a port from which our ancestors set off for more distant shores: the caves of the Dordogne Valley in France; southeastern Turkey where they built monumental structures; a monastery in Georgia that sits atop ancient human remains; a Neanderthal burial pit in the mountains of Spain; and the virgin forests of central Africa, where elephant-hunters still roam. These places are all part of the same story, the same human quest.

Our exciting journey, like every story that uses archeological methods, will take us from the extremely distant past to relatively recent history. From a picnic on the shores of a lake 1.5 million years ago to the mysterious stone circles and sun-worshipping rituals a mere 5,000 or 6,000 years ago. But this is not a linear story; there is no central path with a clear destination. It has twists and turns, surprising shortcuts, and long pauses when nothing of particular note seems to happen. Human evolution is like that: directionless and rather haphazard. This complicates any attempt to tell its story, throwing in plenty of surprises and misunderstandings that we shall try to decipher together.

It is no coincidence that we can make this journey into the heart of the Middle East by visiting stations on both sides of the Jordan Valley. After all, this was a prehistoric corridor connecting the continent of Africa with Europe and Asia. The humans who walked out of the heart of Africa roughly two million years ago had to pass through this land. They stopped there, hunted there, and left their footprints all over. The earliest solid evidence of human use of fire was found north of the Sea of Galilee. It is likely that Neanderthals met members of our own species, *Homo sapiens*, on the slopes of Mount Carmel. They not only bumped into them—they probably also exchanged genes. Hunter-gatherers became farmers there long before almost anywhere else on earth. They built a tall tower there, long before the word "tower" was coined. And there was plenty of action—it was never boring.

Our starting point is one of great respect for our ancestors. Not just because we are abusing the only planet we have while they took much better care of it, but for the simple reason that they were here for a *very long time*. Tens and hundreds of thousands of years, in fact, during which they reached every corner of the planet, crossed mountains and valleys, survived grueling ecological crises, and yet never set their sights too high and always made do with what nature had to offer. Here and there, they too, like us, went a bit far. They hunted more than necessary, crafted more and bigger tools than they needed, quarreled with each other, and probably also ate each other. But all in all, in the grand scheme of things—let's say, in the two million years of human existence—we must doff our caps to them. Or at least learn a thing or two from the fascinating stories of all those who were here before us.

We should also doff our figurative caps to all those who shoved their spades in the right places, crawled into mysterious caves, and painstakingly sifted through tons of dirt, all in the hope of finding something truly important. These archeologists' stories are no less captivating than those of the objects of their inquiry. Knowledgeable, persistent, audacious, and meticulous, they were all titans in their fields, and their momentous discoveries will appear throughout our journey.

We have chosen to interrupt your reading experience as little as possible and have made every effort to purge this book of scientific jargon, which by its nature is not user-friendly. We have skipped many findings and nuggets of information to be able to present big ideas, archeological heroes, and a narrative full of unexpected twists and turns. At the end of the book, you can find the references to the sources we have quoted from and recommendations for further reading on topics we will certainly not have time to do justice to as we plow ahead on our journey.

Finally, one essential clarification: prehistory is a dynamic field. What was once accepted and agreed on two decades ago has since been revised at least once, if not twice. What was orthodoxy a century ago has since been called completely into question. And even this is up for debate and might change at any time. Not long ago, every schoolchild learned that *Homo sapiens* left Africa 60,000 years ago. That has since been updated to 100,000 years ago, and then to 150,000 and even 300,000 years before our time. There were probably several exoduses, not just one. And who is to say that humanity only emerged from Africa? Perhaps human beings returned to Africa from somewhere else before making their famous, fateful, final exodus from Africa?

You will find many more question marks in this book than exclamation marks, although here and there we do state some facts with conviction. We shall probably live to regret some of them. Maybe even the one about the fragment of a swan's wing found deep inside a prehistoric cave.

That's it. Let's get started.

CHAPTER 1
BORN TO ROAM
1.5 million years ago

From Ubeidiya in Israel to Dmanisi in eastern Georgia

When was humankind born? Where did it leave its first fingerprints? What exhilarating discoveries were made in the fields of a kibbutz near the Sea of Galilee? And what does all this have to do with the backache that so many of us suffer from?

It's pleasant here, in the Jordan Valley, especially in winter. This was particularly true in 2020 when, despite forecasts of a long drought and talk of global warming, there was a bewildering amount of unexpected winter rain. The Sea of Galilee was filling up like a jug under a gushing tap. During our weekend field trip alone, the water rose another 13cm (5in). Parking lots flooded, and the lake swamped picnic tables that had been dozens of feet from the water's edge the year before. The Jordan River was practically frothing, the surrounding hills were green, and it was easy to imagine that this area must have looked much like this 1.5 million years ago.

It's a tempting thought, but one that does not even come close to the sheer abundance, beauty, and raw wilderness that existed here in the distant past. Herds of elephants roamed this terrain; hippopotamuses wallowed in the deep waters; and mammoths migrated through the natural passageways along the Jordan Rift Valley. Leopards prowled through the dense thickets, lying in wait for prey. So did lions and bears. The flora was evergreen, the waters deep and fresh. There was once a great lake here, alongside

1

a network of swamps, rivers, and sprawling grasslands. Dozens of bird species swooped onto the meadows, toads croaked, and deer gamboled at ease and munched on the luscious vegetation. Imagine a diverse African nature reserve, then multiply it a hundredfold to come close to picturing what existed here long ago. It was a kind of Garden of Eden, including Adam and Eve and even the snake. Several species of snakes, in fact.

In the late 1950s, Izzy Marimski, who was a member of Kibbutz Afikim (a cooperative community established on socialist and Zionist principles) was searching for suitable land to cultivate tomatoes and zucchini on. The banks of the Jordan River, with their fertile soil and constant sunlight from the southeast, seemed like a promising place for growing winter crops at a time when market prices were sky high. Marimski was an extremely knowledgeable and curious man—he still is, at the age of over eighty. Waiting for the right time to plow and sow the land, he wandered around and found an abundance of river snails and fossils. When he saw huge deer antlers poking out of the ground, he realized that this was very unusual. Deer had not roamed this land for thousands of years.

Further exploration revealed many other zoological remains, which were similarly intriguing because of their size. He also found stone tools, leaving him with no doubt that this was all very ancient. But exactly *how* ancient, he did not yet know.

Marimski packed his discoveries into wooden crates and sent them to Professor Moshe Stekelis at the Prehistoric Archeology Department of the Hebrew University in Jerusalem. Back then, and for many years thereafter, Stekelis was known as the leading expert on the prehistory of Israel. In the mid-1930s, Stekelis collaborated with René Neuville, the French consul general in Jerusalem and a certified archeologist, on a dig at Qafzeh Cave near Nazareth. Together with the British archeologist Francis Turville-Petre, Stekelis discovered and excavated Kebara Cave on Mount Carmel, which was later found to contain a well-preserved Neanderthal skeleton. It was nicknamed Moshe, after the man who began the explorations.

with a stable trunk and a main branch, but more like a brambly bush that developed in different directions.

It is tempting to try to draw an imaginary line between chimpanzees and us, but this would be an impossible and fundamentally fruitless endeavor. Evolution is a messy process, devoid of any direction, purpose, or destination. Different species of more-or-less upright hominids coexisted, flourished, and declined cheek-by-jowl. All but one of them disappeared, like many other species. Just as there are different kinds of leopards and different kinds of whales, there were once different kinds of humans. At a certain point over two million years ago, it is likely that six human species existed side by side in Africa. And like the many kinds of leopards and elephants, not all survived.

To the credit of *Homo habilis*, it possessed a slightly larger brain than the other upright species and it also seems to have been the first to regularly eat other animals, while most other upright mammals remained herbivorous. *Homo habilis* was also the first creature to leave its mark on the prehistoric landscape, through shaped stone tools and animal bones snapped in half from extracting bone marrow, a well-known prehistoric delicacy. Archeology, therefore, begins with *Homo habilis*. The only things that predate it are fossils scattered across open land.

Slightly under two million years ago, this story took a major turn. Specifically, in the direction of significant changes in the size of the human brain. After hundreds of thousands of years when our brain developed at the same pace as the brains of other mammals of the same genus—almost imperceptible changes of a few millimeters—the human brain experienced a sudden growth spurt. In just a few thousand or tens of thousands of years, this organ almost doubled its size. The human brain expanded at an astonishing pace into an energy-guzzling but sophisticated multi-tasking machine. Much had already happened in the prehistoric world, but it is in that epoch in Africa that our story truly begins—a story whose major developments, impressive and destructive alike, we shall trace throughout the course of this book.

There is still no conclusive explanation for why this happened: why did *Homo erectus*'s brain grow so much? There are many hypotheses, but none is backed by any empirical evidence. One of the most plausible theories was proposed by the evolutionary biologist Richard Dawkins, the author of the bestselling book *The Selfish Gene*. Dawkins argues that around two million years ago, humans underwent an "arms race" between our "hardware" (the human brain, in this computer analogy) and our "software" (our use of language, which quickly became more complex and widespread). This required the physical brain to constantly expand so it could cope with the "updates," just as a computer regularly needs updating as programs become increasingly sophisticated. Professor Yoel Rak of Tel Aviv University's Department of Anatomy and Anthropology is one of the world's foremost scholars of human evolution and, in his tantalizing lectures, he not only highlights Dawkins's theory but kicks himself for not thinking of it sooner himself. This idea is undoubtedly brilliant.

As the human brain grew, the human jawline shrank, and the digestive system seems to have also contracted and adapted itself to consuming calories from animal-based foods. We gained prominent noses and later a distinctive chin, shared by no other species. The human body also became bigger and taller and, in fact, we are extremely similarly proportioned to our direct ancestor, *Homo erectus*. This seems to be the reason why many of us suffer from backache and joint pains—the result of genes that acclimatized to climbing up trees and never fully adapted to walking on two legs.

At this point, our distant ancestors started to do some incredible things—two in particular: crafting tools and departing from Africa. It is true that even earlier some hominids were able to make tools but, with the development of the hardware—the brain—came a major technological upgrade. While their predecessors, like other human apes, knew how to use flints to crack open nuts or bones or to use sharpened branches to extract hidden sources of food, the new or refined species of humans developed genuine stone-tool-making technologies. And these were technologies that shared clear, uniform, and enduring characteristics over an exceedingly long timeframe. As for the exodus from Africa, modern-day scholars believe that *Homo habilis* had probably already left Africa and reached as far as central Europe and even China. But large-scale movement, a fully-fledged migration over hundreds of thousands of years, and a discernible presence all across Africa, Asia, and Europe— these were almost certainly the singular achievements of *Homo erectus*, the human species that the researcher Dubois identified as far away as the islands of Indonesia. And then there was the much earlier evidence from Ubeidiya, which Stekelis was about to reveal to the world.

***

The reasons for the exodus of *Homo erectus* from Africa have not been sufficiently investigated and there is no agreed answer to this riddle. But there are several decent hypotheses: the population expansion of a successful species enlarging its territorial footprint; climate change, which dramatically reduced the natural habitat available to this human species; and curiosity and a natural impulse to roam resulting from the growth of the brain and the increasingly impressive cognitive abilities of this first traveler and explorer in human history.

Each of these hypotheses is supported and rejected in part by the evidence, and none can perfectly explain the movement of *Homo erectus* and its broad dispersal across the planet. Of all the proposed triggers, there is one that probably did more than any other to spur this mass exodus from the continent where humanity was born: disease.

The continent of Africa was, and remains, a paradise for viruses. It was a veritable incubator for the accelerated growth of zoonotic diseases (originating in animals) such as plague, brucellosis, anthrax, and many other nasty pathogens. As soon as early humans searched for fresher pastures and walked away from areas riven with illnesses and infections, they found themselves less riddled with the parasites that had made their lives hell. Moreover, viral diseases (such as measles, whooping cough, and smallpox) need dense concentrations of people to flourish—communities of at least tens of thousands of people. Unlike the modern world, where people pass non-stop through airports, conference centers, stadiums, trains, and resorts around the world, in prehistoric times nobody hopped over to London for the weekend or to Italy for a skiing holiday. This book was written during the difficult period of the COVID-19 pandemic, caused by another zoonotic disease—this time possibly made in China—so we can all appreciate the value of leaving our troubles behind by moving somewhere new. The further early humans strayed from problematic terrain, the more their chances of survival improved. Nevertheless, even in the areas that early humans left—modern-day Ethiopia, Kenya, and Tanzania—life did not exactly stop.

In any case, many early humans left Africa and took their reasons with them. Step by step (that's another skill that *Homo erectus* acquired: the ability to walk slowly over long distances), mile by mile, they walked and walked until around 1.5 million years ago they reached more or less the spot where Izzy Marimski bumped into the professor from Jerusalem.

Professor Stekelis did not show up alone to his surprise encounter with Marimski. Walking with him through Kibbutz Afikim were Leo Picard, one of the leading geologists in Israel, a world expert in hydrology, and the Israel Prize for Life Sciences laureate of 1958, and Eitan Tchernov, a young and promising zoologist, one of the founders of the International Council for Archaeozoology.

On that day in the 1950s, the three men squeezed into a jeep and followed Marimski to the agricultural fields that had sprouted some revolutionary archeological findings. They were so excited by what they saw that the young kibbutz member had to run after his honored guests as they trampled the green saplings on their way to the slopes that had revealed the presence and activity of early humans. *Very* early humans—*Homo erectus.*

Stekelis understood at once that he had been presented with the discovery of a lifetime. He dropped everything else that he was doing and focused on Ubeidiya. It was clear to him that this was one of the earliest and richest prehistoric sites in the world. But the excavations proved to be an especially challenging project, even for an experienced archeologist like him and an accomplished geologist like Picard.

Archeological sites are usually structured like layer cakes: on the top is whipped cream, below which is a layer of meringue, and below that is hazelnut nougat, and so on and so on until you bite into the biscuit—or bedrock—at the bottom. Strip away one layer, and you reach the older layer beneath it. The hazelnut nougat is older than the meringue; the meringue is older than the whipped cream. But in Ubeidiya, the archeological layers were not stacked neatly on top of each other. They were sloped at sharp angles, like our layer cake would look if someone squeezed it at both ends. And that's exactly what had happened there—later tectonic activity had compressed, creased, and lifted layers that had once been buried deep underground. Layers that humans who looked rather like us once lived on, long before the compression process began. Thanks to this tectonic activity, these hidden layers had come to the surface. Now, Stekelis had to find a way to conduct a scientific excavation diagonally.

The scholars used heavy diggers to create exploratory channels and progressed horizontally rather than vertically, as in most archeological sites. These holes looked more like windows on the side of a building than excavations to reach its foundations. They revealed that Ubeidiya was a fairly large archeological site, defying expectations about this prehistoric era (the very early Paleolithic period). Early humans existed there and left behind clear signs of their presence. This place once supported a large population who crafted many tools, ate many animals, and most importantly kept returning to the same familiar spot. You could almost compare them to a modern family who goes back to the same lakeside holiday home every summer vacation. The early humans found their favorite place and refused to go elsewhere—even after a couple of thousand years of repeated visits.

Among the archeological layers at Ubeidiya are strata of sediment that suggest this area was occasionally transformed from a lake into a river, and when this happened the local humans had to look for somewhere new to decamp to. When the lake returned, so did they. The jumble of archeological and geological layers descends to a depth of more than 30m (98ft), representing tens and maybe even hundreds of thousands of years of activity. People back then were stubborn and maybe even glued to their land. Just like us.

The summer after the exploratory dig at Ubeidiya, an archeological camp was set up at the site, and delegations of students and volunteers pitched their tents in an allocated section of the kibbutz. Marimski's recollections of this period are extremely vivid: "There was a warm, romantic atmosphere, with lots of interactions, if you catch my drift. Volunteers, and especially lady volunteers, poured in from all over, and in the evenings, everyone sat around the campfire and stuff happened. It was definitely special." Photographs from the first archeological seasons hint at what this charming man hosting us in his modest apartment is talking about: young women (and men) in bathing suits standing on ladders, holding little hammers, and exposing prehistoric tools, which capture the mood perfectly.

The ancient tools discovered in the many digs were made of solid limestone, flint, and basalt: knives made of sharp-tipped flints and ball-shaped tools known as spheroids in the archeological jargon. These were all large instruments; some were fairly coarse, while other, more refined tools were almost identical to those previously unearthed at the Olduvai Gorge in Tanzania and considered the oldest of their kind in the world (dated to 1.8 million years ago). Stekelis had a good reason for calling them "the Israeli variant of Oldowan tradition." Louis

Leakey, one of the world's preeminent prehistorians, who had discovered in Tanzania the earliest human families, visited Ubeidiya and confirmed the identification and classification of these findings.

There were also more sophisticated tools: double-sided, sharp hand axes, which are the most intriguing prehistoric stone tools and will receive the attention they deserve in the next chapter. In Ubeidiya, these were still in their early development stage—a prototype before they became mass produced. Izzy Marimski himself has one extremely impressive example, wrapped in nylon, which he displays next to framed photos of his grandchildren.

One of the defining features of hunter-gatherer societies was their persistent production of these tools throughout the ages and around the world. This is a good way to track and identify the migration routes of traditional societies because they carry with them tools and technologies brought from "home." It stands to reason that like modern butchers, *Homo erectus* had their own set of knives: a cutting knife, a carving knife, a skinning knife, and a meat mallet. If so, then we are talking about culture and tradition, and even organized systems for communicating information and knowledge. Generations of *Homo erectus* had their own tool-crafting methods, which they used for nearly two million years. Quite a success, in evolutionary terms.

However, the most tantalizing discoveries at Ubeidiya were zoological. There was an incredible abundance of animal remains: aurochs, rhinoceroses, monkeys, and terrifying saber-toothed tigers, which certainly scared the living daylights out of the people who lived there. There were also different species of elephants and fallow deer; a range of wild horses, pigs, and hyenas; and at least one species each of giraffe and bear. Hordes of hippopotamuses once inhabited the swamps near the lake, and if anyone had gone fishing in its waters, they would have pulled out a smorgasbord of water creatures, especially meaty catfish. Modern-day nature reserves could only dream of hosting such exotic and abundant wildlife.

There were also nomadic human beings, and if we could have asked them to list the animal species in the region, they would have probably included themselves: monkeys, leopards, elephants—and us. The humans who kept circling back to Ubeidiya hundreds of thousands of years ago did not think that they were the center of the world, and definitely not the crowning glory of creation. No more so than deer, bears, snakes, and scorpions. They were all living beings, which somehow got along in the same environment. They all ate and got eaten. These people must have asked themselves questions like: will that herd of bison stop for a drink at the lake in front of us? Will that pride of lionesses lying in wait for the bison manage to catch their prey? Will these predators leave us any meat, or just broken bones?

With all due respect to the developed brains and motor skills of *Homo erectus*, they still occupied a relatively low position in the food chain compared to other predators. They were probably also aware of their place and accepted their fate with a willingness that allowed them to adapt and survive. "They knew they were meat," writes the American culture critic and author Barbara Ehrenreich in an article about how Paleolithic humans saw the world, "and they also seemed to know that they knew they were meat—meat that could think."

***

Moshe Stekelis passed away in 1967 and his faithful student Ofer Bar-Yosef stepped into his big shoes as the manager of the Ubeidiya excavations. If Stekelis had laid the foundations of prehistoric research in Israel, then it was Bar-Yosef who was the contractor and built the framework of local Paleolithic research. (Sadly, he died during the writing of this book.) He was a brilliant and entertaining man—a member of the American Academy of Arts and Sciences and a professor of anthropology at Harvard University—who knew how to captivate a crowd. Much of Bar-Yosef's research, which began with the findings at Ubeidiya, focused on movement and migration during the Paleolithic era: who hit the road, when, where they went, and where they settled well over a million years ago.

Trying to follow the movement of early humans and to record their precise routes over such long timespans is enough to give anyone a headache. The reams of data gathered from various sites around Asia and Africa are not all equally credible and, in any case, the dating is often imprecise or unclear. In Pakistan, for example, a human stone tool was supposedly discovered and dated to 2.4 million years ago(!), but it is highly doubtful whether it really was made by humans. It might just be a piece of rock that fell off a cliff—and the dating is even more dubious. In South Asia, stone tools were reportedly discovered and dated to 1.6–1.8 million years ago, but this is equally doubtful. ("Doubtful" is an adjective commonly used to describe archeological research, especially in the context of someone else's work. But not your own.)

As for the timing of the exodus from Africa, Bar-Yosef's theory posits three main waves of migration. He proposes that the earliest took place some 1.6–1.8 million years ago and brought with it the sharp tools discovered in Ubeidiya. Another wave followed, apparently 1.4 million years ago; and the third wave took place a mere 800,000 years ago, exporting much more advanced stone tools. But the waters get muddied even further, because there were also later reverse waves of migration, from east to west—from Asia to Africa. It's tempting to say that humans started getting homesick after hundreds of thousands of years abroad.

In his prolific studies, Bar-Yosef repeatedly emphasizes the importance of dispersals from the viral hotspots in Africa as a major driver of *Homo erectus*'s success: "Once humans succeeded in crossing the disease-plagued belts of Africa, the chance of survival for many more members of their groups rose steeply."

Unfortunately, no physical remains of *Homo erectus* have been discovered at Ubeidiya apart from a single tooth and a vertebra. This is obviously disappointing but matches findings at many other archeological sites around the world, where the same early humans lived and settled. Archeologists have discovered tools, evidence of human activity, and animal bones—but no direct trace of the people who ate these animals or got eaten by them. In his book *A Short History of Nearly Everything*, the author Bill Bryson writes that if all known remains conclusively attributed to *Homo erectus* were to rise from the dead, "they wouldn't fill a school bus." There were many thousands of them living hundreds of thousands of years ago, but it seems they were careful not to leave any traces of their lives. Or maybe we haven't been looking hard enough.

***

In the early 1990s, something massive happened in the world of prehistory. An archeological expedition discovered the fossilized remains of early humans from 1.7–1.8 million years ago. Surprisingly, these fossils were found during excavations under the foundations of a medieval Orthodox cathedral, and not in Africa, but in the town of Dmanisi in Georgia, in the Caucasus. The archeologists had set out to find an ancient altar or a holy cross but instead discovered the ancient ancestors of the Son of God. At Dmanisi, which has since become a center of Paleolithic research and a world heritage site, archeologists found a lower jaw with a complete set of teeth, skull fragments, and other skeletal remains. In later excavations, no fewer than five early human skulls were unearthed at the site, more than at any other early prehistoric site in the world.

Professor Yoel Rak recalls that, like many others, he was initially skeptical about these findings in Georgia. But when he was invited there as an expert witness and held one of the skulls, his doubts disappeared: this had once been a human head. Not exactly *Homo erectus*, but extremely similar. Named *Homo georgicus*, it was a slightly earlier variety of *Homo erectus*. Like his traveling companions—elephants, to name but one—this human species had also arrived from Africa one day—and not aboard a flight from Addis Ababa to Tbilisi, that's for sure.

With the discoveries in Dmanisi, an even earlier site than Ubeidiya had been found—and this time with human remains—resulting in its crown as the earliest known site of human activity outside of Africa being torn away. Archeologists from Germany, France, Spain, and the United States descended on Georgia and, quite rightly, poured money into the site. By contrast, Ubeidiya is today unjustly reduced to a site of thorns and thistles, and there isn't even a sign pointing to this place, which until recently was considered the oldest human settlement outside of Africa. Nevertheless, many scholars think it is a mistake to date Ubeidiya to 1.4 million years ago solely from the tools discovered there, and they believe this was a site of much earlier human activity. Even earlier than Dmanisi.

So, everything remains wide open. One can at least hope that a path will be paved for visitors to Ubeidiya, and perhaps a sign proudly stating: "HUMANS LIVED HERE OVER 1.5 MILLION YEARS AGO."

Excavations at Ubeidiya, notice ladders and swimsuits

CHAPTER 2

THE FAT-HUNTERS

750,000 years ago

Were elephants on the prehistoric menu? Why should you never mock a hyena? What is the handicap principle, and what has it got to do with prehistoric tool-making? And when is conservatism a strength, not a drawback?

A long and patient line of tourists snaked across the plaza in front of the Pompidou Center in Paris. Acrobats, mime artists, and flame swallowers took advantage of this waiting period to pass around a hat to collect change from visitors in line at the ticket stand. A troupe of Senegalese drummers played on big metal barrels. A young busker won a round of applause for her moving rendition of Adele's "Someone Like You."

This was not the first exhibition to create a buzz and congestion at the entrance of Beaubourg, as Parisians call this museum, but the one that opened in May 2019 was truly exceptional. Even its name was puzzling: "Prehistory: A Modern Enigma." The huge sign that announced the exhibition, draped across the four-story façade of this industrial-looking building, could not help but astonish visitors, presenting them with a remarkable picture: a Paleolithic hand axe dipped in phosphorescent yellow rubber. It was a brilliant combination of an elegant prehistoric tool and a material and color that are standard features of our modern lives.

The exhibit chosen as the iconic symbol of this exhibition was the work of a pair of Israeli designers, Ami Drach and Dov Ganchrow, as part of an artistic dialogue between past and present, between the trademark technology of the prehistoric era and the materials and production methods of the twenty-first century. In one series, Drach and Ganchrow focused on rubber and yellow; in another, they silver-plated stone tools and turned them into fancy dining utensils; in a third series, they used 3-D printing techniques to make a modern axe. All three series were based on the same prehistoric tool—a hand axe.

Hand axes are tools with two sharp flanks and a pointy tip, knapped in such a meticulously symmetrical fashion that you want to display one in your living room or at least hold one in your hand. This is the tool that Izzy Marimski discovered at Ubeidiya and keeps wrapped in nylon next to photos of his grandchildren. This is the tool that was crafted hundreds and thousands of times in exactly the same way, with the same production techniques, practically everywhere on earth that *Homo erectus* reached. This is the tool that defined the Acheulean culture, which began in Africa nearly two million years ago and lasted until roughly 400,000 years ago (and is named after the town of Saint-Acheul in France, where hand axes were first classified). Hand axes are informally known as "Paleolithic Swiss Army knives," to explain not only their multi-functionality but also their established presence in human life. What other tool has been manufactured for hundreds of thousands of years, practically without change?

Not only did the technology behind the hand axe stay the same, but it reached every corner of the Old World. It's as if early humans lugged the templates around with them on their travels, keeping them under lock and key, careful not to deviate from the blueprints. They used a range of materials—basalt, flint, obsidian, limestone, bones—and crafted these hand axes in different sizes, but their basic appearance, structure, and manufacturing methods remained uniform. Hand axes unearthed at Acheulean sites in Boxgrove in England and Bose in China look like they could have come from the same prehistoric factory. That's why the Pompidou Center's curators accepted not only visually impressive exhibits but also those with a clear affinity to the theme of "enigma." The hand axe is probably the most enigmatic of all prehistoric instruments.

So many questions have been asked about hand axes. Why have such huge piles of them—more than could have ever made practical sense—been found at certain sites? Why did early humans make such intricate tools, when it is quite clear that simpler ones could have also done the job? Why was the two-sided symmetry of these tools so important? How can we explain the appearance of some excessively large hand axes, which could not possibly have had any practical use?

Marek Kohn and Steven Mithen, academics from Reading University in England, have explored these questions and came up with a surprising answer: early humans wanted to impress the opposite sex. Kohn and Mithen draw on the "handicap principle," a theory devised by the Israeli zoologists (and husband and wife) Amotz and Avishag Zahavi, who devoted their careers to studying Arabian babblers: a species of bird that lives in groups on acacia trees in desert areas. Based on their tenacious observations, the Zahavis proved that animals promote themselves in their group hierarchies by deliberately handicapping themselves. In their hypothesis, it is not the strongest or most adaptable that survive, but those that *publicize themselves* as such: those that openly flaunt their ability to burden themselves, overcome difficulties, and prosper. This is how animals project that they have good genes, which are fit for use and should be handed down to offspring. And this is why Arabian babblers, for example, spend hours on "guard duty," refusing to vacate their posts for the next "watchmen," insist on helping each other, and even forgo food so as not to be considered greedy or needy. This is also why peacocks fan out their tails, which impedes their movement and exposes them to predators but also makes them look beautiful and creates an impression that boosts their chances of finding a mate and procreating. Just like how some men blow money on dates and drive expensive fancy cars.

Kohn and Mithen claim that *Homo erectus* invested exceptional efforts to craft hand axes for similar reasons: "Those hominids . . . who were able to make the symmetrical hand-axes may have been preferentially chosen by the opposite sex as mates," write Kohn and Mithen, "just as a peacock's tail may reliably indicate its 'success.'" Hand axes, therefore, were not merely working tools but also *marketing* tools. Prehistoric stonemasons operated under the critical gaze of women, who inspected each man's work and made sure that none passed off another man's hand axe as his own. This might explain the huge number of hand axes at many prehistoric sites. Every man wanted to be a player. The abnormally large hand axes that were too heavy to lift were probably made by the master craftsmen, the alpha males of yesteryear. Women, according to Kohn and Mithen, got by with their own standard hand axes, which they probably made themselves. They had their own virtues. It was the men who had to exert themselves in the evolutionary race.

This is certainly an original theory, which probably explains something about finding a mate in the prehistoric world. And yet, the conventional explanation for the mystery of hand axes is also the simplest and most obvious: they were highly efficient tools. Hand axes did a much better job than other tools at chopping up large animals, early humans' main source of calories. Only when this mode of existence changed did the technology used by humans also change. (It's a change we will come to in Chapter 4 of this book, around 300,000 years on from now.)

***

Hand axes have also been found at the site of the Daughters of Jacob's Bridge, in the northern Jordan Valley (known in Hebrew as Gesher Benot Ya'aqov). These are not any old hand axes, but ones made mostly of basalt as opposed to flint, the most commonly used material in the region. Naama Goren-Inbar, who has meticulously and efficiently run seven archeological seasons there, and whose research elevated the site to global scientific importance, says that the choice of basalt seems to suggest that the locals were recent immigrants from Africa. Their group had come from the cradle of humanity and continued making hand axes using materials that were familiar from home. Goren-Inbar unearthed and identified an enormous array of early foodstuffs in the archeological layers at Daughters of Jacob's Bridge. She found thirteen different species of fish (mostly carp, which grew up to 2m (6.5ft) long and were grilled on site); fifty-five species of plants, fruits, bulbs, and edible and nutritious grains; acorns, raspberries, hollyhock leaves, and Christ's thorn jujube to name just a few of the distinctive ingredients in the Paleolithic diet there. Nevertheless, their preference, says Goren-Inbar, was for elephants, hippopotamuses, and fallow deer. These were three delicacies, according to their presence among local bone finds. One of these three, in our opinion, seems to have been in highest demand: elephants. They were perfect bundles of food, traipsing around the area.

The massive change in *Homo erectus*'s brains, which made the species what it was (and in time, produced us), required greater sources of energy. The human brain has an almost insatiable appetite for calories, and since the digestive system also consumes large amounts of energy, the evolutionary solution to balance the two was to suppress one (digestion) at the expense of the other (the brain). Once this prehistoric species' stomach shrank, plants, leaves, and seeds no longer satisfied its needs. It became dependent on richer, denser, and more easily available sources of energy. In menu terms: meat and animal fat. Especially lots of fat.

It was a simple calculation: one gram of meat was worth on average four calories. One gram of fat, however, gave us nine calories—more than double. Unlike plants and lean meat, the consumption of fat incurred no digestive costs, as every gram that early humans ate was theirs to use. No other foodstuff is as efficient. It's no coincidence that modern-day hunter-gatherers are crazy about fat and appreciate and love its taste more than any other food (with the possible exception of honey, because who doesn't have a sweet tooth?). Fat is rich in calories, easy to digest, and extremely yummy.

Modern humans are seriously constrained when it comes to extracting calories from meat alone. If you try to eat nothing but meat, all day every day, you won't remain with us for long. We are advised to eat a balanced diet mainly because of the inefficiencies in our digestive system, especially the liver, which is supposed to expel toxins. Given these shortcomings, we can only squeeze one-third of our recommended daily calories from meat alone. The other two-thirds must come from other sources, namely plants or fat.

The overconsumption of low-fat meat can lead to hunger, malnutrition, and even death. "Rabbit starvation" (or "protein poisoning") is the phenomenon whereby people who eat nothing but lean rabbit meat end up meeting a similar fate to their prey. It's inadvisable, no matter how much you like eating bunnies. Since we are physiologically extremely similar to our distant ancestors *Homo erectus*, the same protein limitations probably also affected them. Despite the prevalence of game in the prehistoric world, early humans also needed the same nutritional balance between meat and fat. This is where proboscideans—elephants and mammoths—enter, or rather stampede into, the picture.

Elephants and mammoths were the largest walking fat reserves in the natural world. Their long gestation, nursing, and childrearing periods required them to keep a stable supply of fat all year round. Prehistoric elephants had an average caloric potential of five million calories, split equally between lean meat and fat. In other words, the fat of a single elephant was an adequate food supply for ten people for 100 days. If we add the lean meat from the same carcass, then one elephant provided them with enough calories for 200 days. Paleolithic hunters worked this out long before us and aimed their spears at the most economically worthwhile targets to sustain their existence.

These scientific insights, and their gastronomic implications, form the basis of Miki Ben-Dor's research. Ben-Dor stumbled into this field quite by accident, looking for an escape from decades of work in the bromine industry. He signed up for creative writing classes, concluded that he would never make it as a poet, then roamed the corridors of his university. When he opened the door to a lecture on hunter-gatherers, he realized that this was what he was looking for. That's what he wanted to do: to get as far away as possible from manufacturing and transporting chemicals across the industrial world. "We are hunter-gatherers in our genes, and we've been plunged into a time and place that are not quite right for us," Ben-Dor says as we wait for our espressos at the cafeteria of the humanities faculty at Tel Aviv University. "Hunter-gatherers are noble people, perfectly suited to their environments—much more than we are."

From studying hunter-gatherers and prehistoric archeology, Ben-Dor progressed to the subject of Paleolithic nutrition, started a blog about it, and became something of a missionary preaching against conventional dietary advice. "My eyes were opened to the catastrophe of overconsuming carbohydrates instead of meat," he explains. "The subject gripped me, and I decided I had to work in this field." And that's what he does, with gusto. When he read about the importance of elephants at sites where *Homo erectus* lived, his grand theory came together: "The whole of human evolution is based on fat. Early humans were fat-hunters."

If we want to understand what enabled the human brain to grow in volume two million years ago—what fuel propelled humanity forward—then fat hacked from large animals must be one of our first and primary explanations.

One archeological finding from the excavations at Daughters of Jacob's Bridge presents a fascinating scene from the story of early humans' interactions with elephants. On a large block of basalt from which hand axes were crafted, archeologists found a thick branch of an oak tree. On the branch was the shattered skull of a young or female elephant. Only the base of the skull had survived in its entirety; the other pieces were scattered all around. Someone had made the effort to take the skull there, place it on a hard surface, and not just smash it but continue to break it open to reach its innards. This was a coordinated venture, performed by several people. They had to find their prey, decapitate it, drag something that weighed over 200kg (440lbs) to this place, position the skull, balance it, crush it with great force, and take it apart. This was a chain of events that undoubtedly required basic communication between the participants: "You hold this, you lift that, and now—all together!" Most researchers maintain that humans still lacked a coherent language, and maybe even words, but it is hard to see how an elephant skull showed up there without the perpetrators using any kind of dialogue or social communication. Or even a real language, for that matter.

Goren-Inbar and her team of researchers propose that this whole complicated enterprise had a single goal: to scoop out the elephant's brain, which weighed around 6kg (13lbs). It was surely a tasty and worthwhile treat. But what about all the other bits that came with the elephant's head? What about its tongue or the fatty tissue on its temples? These were also sources of food, and modern-day hunter-gatherers would eat them in a heartbeat if they got their hands on an elephant. Elephant skulls are made of spongy bone, full of liquid fat, and early humans probably pulverized them to extract this hidden energy reserve. Whichever way you look at it, elephants were caloric treasure troves.

How did such a treasure trove fall into the hands of prehistoric humans? That's a tricky question, which, again, like many other issues in prehistoric research, lacks a conclusive answer. There are two camps: those who assume that all hominid species before *Homo sapiens* were inferior to us and had weaker abilities, and those who believe the opposite and rate the capabilities of early humans highly. The first camp paints a picture without any serious hunting, in which *Homo erectus* was totally dependent on other predators' leftovers. In other words, they were scavengers. The second camp argues that the same humans who made sophisticated stone tools had many other known aptitudes and were probably also capable of hunting elephants. In the absence of archeological evidence until recently supporting either side, all that remained for both camps was to double down on their positions and wage bitter arguments like only academics can.

Torralba, a large Paleolithic site on the road from Madrid to Zaragoza, offers an excellent example of the nature and power of this long-running academic dispute. The site was first unearthed in the early twentieth century by Enrique de Aguilera, the Marquess of Cerralbo, who found no fewer than 500 fragments of prehistoric elephant bones. These remains, which were tightly packed together next to other animal remains, aroused tremendous curiosity and raised questions about the circumstances of the elephants' death. The obvious explanation was that humans were to blame. In the 1960s, an American archeologist by the name of Francis Clark Howell arrived at Torralba and joined forces with local archeologists for a comprehensive and ambitious excavation. Howell found a cluster of hand axes next to the elephant remains, connected the dots, and proposed a theory that this was the site of not just a hunt, but an elephant massacre. Animated nature documentaries that depict prehistoric hunters prodding herds of mammoths or elephants off clifftops with their spears were probably inspired by Howell's graphic impressions.

Lewis Binford, one of the twentieth century's preeminent archeologists, was a brilliant yet merciless man when it came to what he saw as professional follies. He re-examined Howell's findings and crushed them to a fine powder. Having transformed the world of archeology by laying the foundations for an original approach called "processual archeology," Binford showed that Howell had made a complete mess of findings that were not necessarily connected: the hand axes had come from far away, the elephants had sunk into the primordial mud, and the fractures on the bones were from the teeth of the predators that had left human beings some leftovers. There was no massacre, not even a hunt. Obviously, this did not put an end to the argument. Howell tried to defend his honor, other scholars jumped into the fray, and at least one paper has been written about each elephant bogged down in the mud of Torralba. If not more.

In the first decades of the twenty-first century, evidence has piled up in support of the case that *Homo erectus* (and perhaps their predecessors) were able hunters. The most significant piece of evidence comes from Schöningen in Germany, where archeologists unearthed wooden spears dating back to 300,000 years ago. Next to these spears were the remains of horses and elephants—many horses and quite a few elephants. The spears were mightily impressive: long and sharp. Olympic javelin throwers conducted an experiment with replicas and showed that they were exceptionally lethal. The people who used them hundreds of thousands of years ago were skilled hunters and were probably quite able to get by without favors from satiated predators. Similar spears have been found at sites from around the same period, and if organic material did not decompose so quickly, they too could probably be connected to active hunting. As we work on the English edition of this book, a new study reveals direct evidence of elephant-hunting by Neanderthals living in modern-day Germany 125,000 years ago. According to the study, mature male elephants were hunted and butchered, supplying human groups with tons of meat and fat. This is just a single new study, but it might provide the smoking gun, or at least some smoke, in this debate.

Moreover, studies conducted mainly in the Olduvai Gorge, which as we have mentioned was the cradle of humanity (see page 10), pointed to cut-marks caused by stone tools on the inside of animal ribs. According to the researchers, these marks attest to the removal of the prized internal organs, such as hearts and livers. Predators would not have easily given up on these innards, if at all, to leave them for the next in line. That means that someone got there first. Someone who must have used stone tools and presumably knew how to hunt. A human: *Homo erectus.*

Adult elephants have no natural predators. No creature but a human would dare to hunt them. It is possible, however, that the elephant in the northern Jordan Valley died a natural death and the diners there managed to reach it before other predators. This would have been no trivial matter, and a showdown with other scavengers probably filled the air with clouds of dust and blood-curdling battle cries. Clans of hyenas would have been humans' top competitors for this bounty.

Humans and hyenas are inveterate foes. Both trace their roots to the African savanna, and both were pushed into the same habitats and maintained a bitter rivalry for millennia. In her fabulous book *The Unexpected Truth about Animals*, the nature documentary-maker Lucy Cooke gives hyenas back much of the respect they have been unjustly deprived of. Hyenas have a sense of smell 1,000 times more powerful than our own; each clan has its own distinct scent distinguishing it from others; and they are clever and enjoy a rich social life. Cooke joined a field study led by Sarah Benson-Amram, an expert in hyena cognition and communications, who argues that sociality may be the evolutionary mechanism responsible for the high abilities of the hyena. They live in large communities, defend territories hundreds of miles wide and, according to Cooke, hyenas are even more tribal than football fans. So, a battle over the head of an elephant that dropped dead would have been an especially difficult business—a brawl between hooligans from rival teams.

On the other hand, we can at least assume that *Homo erectus*, who lived some 750,000 years ago, were capable of hunting elephants by themselves. According to Goren-Inbar's research, the Daughters of Jacob's Bridge site was home to humans who were highly skilled, were perfectly familiar with their surroundings, and possessed impressive cognitive and technological abilities (including the use of fire, a hugely important subject, which we shall address soon). Studies of modern-day indigenous groups who still hunt elephants for food demonstrate that this is not a simple task just requiring courage and the use of short-range spears, but that it is definitely possible. Hunting elephants may not be a daily occurrence, and wastefulness is frowned upon by those who live in peace and harmony with the animal kingdom, but as a one-off venture, it is efficient, practical, and extremely valuable. That still applies as much today as it did in the distant past.

***

One interesting find that keeps cropping up at various sites from this period is a hand axe made from elephant bone. The bones that were snapped to extract the marrow were recycled and converted into tools remarkably like those used to carve up the same elephant in the first place. It is hard to believe that this was a random act, with no importance beyond the makers' thriftiness. There was a statement here, one with multiple meanings. These hand axes were quite possibly a solid expression, in both senses of the term, of the cosmological place of elephants in the lives of members of the Acheulean culture. This was the circle of life—humans, elephants, and stones.

Hunter-gatherer societies, past and present, conceive of the world as a synthesis of different entities, human and non-human alike. Animal, plant, and object. Soaring mountains, frothing rivers, living creatures—are all equal and complementary beings. All these beings have rights, desires, and aspirations that must be treated with respect for the world to keep on turning. This is an ontological approach to humanity's place in the world and its relations with others. The centrality of elephants in the world of members of the Acheulean culture might explain why they chose to use their bones to craft tools with such a dominant role in their lives. Hand axes made of elephant bone remained part of an elephant and allowed their users to absorb certain elephant qualities and become, in their minds, part-elephant themselves. This was a profoundly important means of strengthening the relationship between human and beast.

Anthropological research presents a complicated picture of the ancient interplay between human beings and elephants. The Samburu tribes in Kenya believe that elephant trunks are the equivalent of human arms and see a resemblance between elephant udders and human breasts, and between elephant skin and human skin. The Baka, an indigenous pygmy people in Cameroon, explain the similarity between themselves and elephants in terms of their shared love of yams, a sweet root vegetable. The Nayaka people in southern India believe that elephants are almost super-entities and understand the world much like humans. The Nuer people, who live along the Nile in Sudan, believe in a mythological link between humans and elephants, including common ancestors. According to the legend, these shared ancestors had an enormous girl with long teeth. When she grew up, she cut herself off from other humans and knew that in the future, she and her kind would become hunted by them. Before leaving, she left the Nuer people clear hunting instructions: "People will want to kill me for my huge tusks and sweet and fatty flesh. The people I came from will want to hunt me, and you may do so without punishment only if you obey my instructions." For the Nuer, elephant-hunting is a necessary and understandable activity, but one subjected to strict constraints, rooted in the depths of their collective consciousness and founding tribal myth.

In the Congo Basin, there are pygmy groups for whom hunting elephants is part of their basic economy. They live hundreds of miles away from the Nuer in Sudan, but traces of the Nuer ancient myth seem to have permeated their world. They perform intricate and elaborate rituals before, during, and after every hunt to ensure the enforcement of their social and economic conventions about hunting elephants. Jerome Lewis, an anthropologist and environmental activist who is conducting an ongoing field study with the Bayaka people in the Republic of the Congo, describes a case in which one tribesman strayed from the traditional hunting conventions and killed a large number of elephants. After he ignored warnings to desist from this wasteful rampage, the women started snubbing him and refused to cook the meat he brought. This lone hunter met a sorry and painful end: he was expelled from the tribe and cursed that he would meet a silverback gorilla in the jungle. Gorilla or not, he met a swift death.

Needless to say, none of these rules, limitations, or myths is resistant to the ravages of the modern world and the lethal trade in elephant tusks and rhinoceros horns. Cash pulverizes old ways of life; it blinds people and corrupts traditions and cherished beliefs about cosmic relations between human and beast. Only rarely in the modern world are elephants afforded the respect they deserve. One such elephant was Ahmed, born in the 1920s at the Marsabit National Park in northern Kenya. Nicknamed "the king," he was something of a loner for most of his life, and it is said that his tusks were so long that when he wanted to climb a hill, he had to walk backwards in order not to get stuck in the ground. He was an attractive target for hunters, and many bullets hit his thick skin, but Ahmed survived. An emotional letter sent by schoolchildren from across Kenya to their enlightened president, Jomo Kenyatta, saved Ahmed the elephant and officially made him a national treasure. He was placed under armed guard, day and night. Ahmed died at the grand old age of sixty-five, resting like a king on his tusks. This is the pose in which he is displayed in Kenya's Nairobi National Museum.

The story of Ahmed the Kenyan elephant can also serve as a reminder of the great importance of elephants in the lives of hunter-gatherers in the Paleolithic world.

It is hard to say for certain when exactly (and until when exactly) prehistoric hunter-gatherers lived in the region of Daughters of Jacob's Bridge, but we can make an educated guess. The total depth of the layers excavated at the site is 30m (98ft)! That's 30 meters of evidence of recurrent human activity on the shores of a freshwater lake, much like the one that once existed at Ubeidiya. Chronologically, that translates into 100,000 years of human activity. This is an impressively long timespan, throughout which hand axes and elephants had a permanent presence. These were the immutable hallmarks of the Acheulean culture.

For us, modern-day humans, whose fashions change daily and who feel an insatiable urge to constantly upgrade our devices, the technological stasis of *Homo erectus* is unfathomable. Quite inexplicable. If we could go back in time, we might tell them, "Hey, humans! You've crossed continents, climbed mighty mountains, gone to battle with hyenas, and hunted elephants—don't you fancy a change? Don't you want to improve, make progress, and move on to a newer model? Why are you still stuck with that clunky old hand axe?" There is something to these musings, which often appear in books about the Acheulean culture. But it is doubtful whether the people we would question—generations of *Homo erectus*—would have seen things the same way. It is doubtful whether they would have understood what we want from them and why we keep banging on about the importance of progress. They had excellent tools, they had elephants, so what would be the rush? What was wrong with a conservative approach that had always worked well for them?

The combination of hand axes and fat-rich mammals sustained *Homo erectus* for over 1.5 million years. Conservative as they may have been, they reached far and wide, and they lasted much longer on Planet Earth than we *Homo sapiens* might predict that we ourselves will.

A group of contemporary pigmy hunters butchering an elephant in the Congo forest, Africa

CHAPTER 3

MEET THE FLINTSTONES

500,000 years ago

**From the Upper Galilee to the Andes and stone quarries
in southern Ethiopia**

**Why do some people pamper rocks with coca leaves in the
Andes? Who is the "old man" from New Hampshire? And
why is the journey no less important than the destination?**

In the early 1960s, something huge happened in U.S. commercial
television. The ABC network commissioned an animated show
from Hanna-Barbera Productions for a primetime audience.
Not short skits featuring Mickey Mouse or Bugs Bunny, but a
series of thirty-minute episodes about a brand-new family of
characters: the Flintstones, who lived in the fictional town of
Bedrock, and whose possessions were all made of stone (and
some leather and wood), including the morning newspaper
that the Paleolithic paperboy threw every day at their cave
door. The only "anachronism" in this prehistoric landscape is
the cigarettes that Fred Flintstone smoked as he leaned on a
huge rock. With all due respect to flint, Winston Cigarettes, the
main sponsor of the show, made a mint from selling a different
substance altogether.

Until *The Simpsons* came along in the late 1980s, not only
was *The Flintstones* the most profitable animated show in the
history of television but the Flintstones characters themselves
were also one of the most famous fictional families in the world.
The show ran for six seasons, depicting a whole world carved
out of stone.

Stones played a central role in the lives of prehistoric humans. In the absence of sharp nails or teeth, and without exceptional physical abilities, humans invented stone tools to keep themselves alive. It was a solution that allowed them to hunt wild animals, carve the meat that they had hunted, process animal skin for various needs (shelter, clothing, storage containers), chop wood and other plant-based materials, and probably carry out many other activities that we have forgotten are necessary for human existence. Without sharp stone tools, it's doubtful we would have made it more than two steps out of Africa.

On the "to-do list" of the people who woke up every morning hundreds of thousands of years ago, many activities revolved around stones: carrying stones, knapping stones, sculpting stones to exact proportions, fixing stones, recycling stones, etc. But the most important item was finding stones—in particular, finding *the* stone, the most useful kind of stone, the stone that was most suitable for the tasks at hand. The stone that if tapped at the right angle would splinter into hard chips useful for a range of human activities. In short: *flint.* There were obviously other stones lying around, such as granite, obsidian, basalt—and sometimes people used elephant or mammoth bones—but the bread and butter of their industry was flint, which is a hard sedimentary rock with a remarkably consistent chemical composition.

Once, until recently, researchers thought that early humans found their raw materials under their homes—at the entrance to their caves or in a nearby gorge. They went for a stroll, went to the end of the street, picked up promising-looking stones, popped them in their non-existent caveman pockets, and then found a quiet corner and a few spare minutes to knap away. But that was in the past, when even serious and respected archeologists gave little credit to our distant ancestors. It is, or at least was, a typically modern and Western habit to belittle and downplay people who are different. Definitely, if they were last around hundreds of thousands of years ago. But this view is mistaken, certainly when it comes to early humans' deep understanding of their landscape. We modern humans live indoors, go out occasionally on family trips, do ourselves a favor by going on short walks, and venture out to find good restaurants, not flint deposits. But our ancestors lived in the great outdoors 24/7, breathed it in, and understood it. They were the closest prehistoric equivalent to modern geologists or geomorphologists—experts in locating strata of underground rock deposits.

The rocks that "rock up," pardon the pun, on the surface of the earth are exposed to sunlight and temperature changes. Many of them are already cracked, having been buffeted around in the rivers or waterfalls that cast them there. These rocks are second-grade material, which might just be suitable for odd jobs around the house, but not for serious tasks, such as chopping elephant meat. That would require high-quality rock and—unsurprisingly, yet still fairly impressively—our distant ancestors knew exactly how to find these deposits. They understood that exposing an outer stratum of flint would lead them to a wide inner plane of the same rock. Using their finely tuned senses, they connected the dots between the flint boulders they found lying in riverbeds and the possibility that the same rock existed all along both banks of the river, probably for hundreds of meters in either direction right beneath their feet. Hundreds of meters of high-quality flint. And—perhaps most remarkably of all—they knew exactly how to reach it.

Early humans removed layers of rock, descended into the bowels of the earth, and undertook projects that left traces that can still be made out today. They were miners and stonecutters, just as we have in modern life . . . only without sticks of dynamite, hydraulic drills, and trucks to transport their wares.

***

Francis Turville-Petre was perhaps the most interesting prehistorian to have visited Mandatory Palestine (a geopolitical entity that lasted from 1920 until 1948), and he was certainly the one with the most turbulent life. He was openly gay at a time when this was still illegal, and was the boyfriend and lover of the celebrated British poet W. H. Auden. He was also a hedonistic bon-vivant, and an opium and alcohol addict. He won professional acclaim thanks to his excavations of Wadi Amud in the 1920s and his discovery of the skull of a man nicknamed "Galilee Man"—the earliest human remains ever discovered in the Levant, and whose precise dating is still a matter of dispute: did he live 400,000 years ago, or just 200,000 years ago? Anyone with a passing interest in prehistory has probably already heard the story about how this skull was first discovered by the site manager's dog, which ran around with it as if it were a toy bone and not one of the most important discoveries in world archeology. During his days off, of which there were many, Turville-Petre enjoyed hiking around the Upper Galilee with his hyperactive dog, which was how he reached Mount Pua and the unusual stone deposits that covered it. In his book *Researches in Prehistoric Galilee*, he gave the mountain the striking name "Mount of Flint."

Some seventy years later, at the tail-end of the twentieth century, the archeologists Avi Gopher and Ran Barkai (one of the authors of this book) climbed the "Mount of Flint" that had once fascinated Turville-Petre. They were already out of breath from the long hike, but their breath was completely taken away when they realized, after a scholarly inquiry, that the piles of stones Turville-Petre and other backpackers had seen were actually a monumental prehistoric quarry. This was a quarry first operated hundreds of thousands of years ago, with systematic, organized workflows clearing layers of limestone, exposing flint deposits deep underground, preparing surfaces to begin processing this hard material, and deliberately disposing of waste in order not to impede future works. It was a full-blown factory, or rather, an industrial zone. And this was only the first of many discoveries in the area. Just the tip of the iceberg. The tip of the quarry.

Mount Pua soars to an elevation of 700m (2,297ft) between Kibbutz Baram and the picturesque Maronite Christian village of Jish. At the bottom of the mountain snakes the beautiful gorge of Wadi Dishon, an ideal transportation route from the Jordan Valley to the peaks of the Upper Galilee. Nowadays, access to the mountain is via one of the prettiest roads in Israel, the sort of road where during a short drive, there's always someone in the car who can't resist the temptation to shout, "It's just like Switzerland!"

One of the people who take this route every day is Meir Finkel, a senior Israeli military officer. Finkel is the kind of restless person who considers every spare hour without activity to be a waste of precious time. When he realized that he had a few free hours on his hands, he filled them by starting a PhD in archeology, a subject about which he hadn't the faintest clue. In the third or fourth lesson in the introductory course, the students were shown a slide from the quarry at Mount Pua. That weekend, this military strategist-cum-budding archeologist drove to visit his wife's family near the Lebanese border. At one of the turnings on the winding road, Finkel looked up at the mountaintops and saw something that reminded him of a slide from the introductory course: heaps of rubble from a quarry. Not one, nor even two or three. The peaks above Nahal Dishon seemed to be dotted with dozens of piles of rock, just like those at Mount Pua.

On the way back from that family visit, and on many following weekends, Finkel's children ran after him up these mountains as he feverishly documented what would become his new obsession: prehistoric mines and quarries. This would also become the subject of his doctoral thesis and would give a major boost to our understanding of the prevalence of this phenomenon in this region and its importance in human history.

The Wadi Dishon area has been found to contain 25km² (9.7mi²) packed with tens of thousands of piles of rubble from prehistoric quarries. A study of one such heap revealed it contained no fewer than 250,000 flint pieces that had been processed in one way or another by humans. That's a quarter of a million objects human hands had held at one point or another and shattered, broken, knapped, and thrown aside because they were defective or redundant or because it was time for lunch. Whatever the reason, the quantities are inconceivable. This was a vast industrial area that produced an enormous output over tens if not hundreds of thousands of years—a "Paleolithic Flint Depot," as Finkel puts it.

It's safe to assume that the people who came to find these flint deposits hundreds of thousands of years ago were the same ones we met at Ubeidiya and Daughters of Jacob's Bridge. Or rather, not quite the same people, but their descendants. They were members of the *Homo erectus* family who, since marching out of Africa, had already reached every corner of the globe, from western Europe to China and Indonesia. They came, they saw, they conquered; they walked out of Africa, and returned there; and for hundreds of thousands of years, they carried with them the same basic yet efficient technology— the hand axe. Mount Pua and its environs were sites for the mass production of this prehistoric Swiss Army knife, whether to impress potential mates, or to carve up large animals, or probably for both purposes and other essential tasks.

Even if we consider continued human activity over tens and even hundreds of thousands of years, the sheer quantities at the prehistoric quarries of the Upper Galilee make no sense. These cavemen were not manufacturing goods for the entire population of China or India. Hunter-gatherer bands during this period, the Lower Paleolithic, are estimated to have contained a few dozen people each. Between a few hundred to a few thousand people would have inhabited this whole space at any given time. It is hard to understand the massive scale of these quarries from the immediate practical perspective of these prehistoric artisans, not just here but in many other places around the world.

No evidence of protracted settlement has been found at these Galilean masonry sites. The stonemasons and their helpers showed up for a night, maybe two or three, and then returned to wherever they had come from: to their wives, their children, and their assorted hunting jobs. Or perhaps their families came with them. Maybe they met friends here and exchanged vital information as their children sat on their laps and learned how to shift flint boulders and produce flint fragments without hurting their fingers. Some of them came from nearby. In the 1970s, the archeologist Milla Ohel, who was also a sports journalist and children's novelist, unearthed an abundance of Paleolithic settlement sites in the area around those quarries. Most of them were near sources of water, and Ohel argued that migrating storks were convenient and available targets for Paleolithic hunter-gatherers.

Other early humans departed from various places in the Jordan Valley, climbed up Wadi Dishon, and hiked up to the quarries at the top of the mountain. The journey itself was significant. In certain modern-day tribal cultures, the effort needed to get one's hands on material from a quarry is no less important, if not more important, than the material itself. For Aboriginal Australians, for example, this is a rite of passage for children and a ritual obligation for adults. The journey is a statement of prestige, honor, ability, and of course physical achievement: proof that you've made it. That you've been there. That you've reached your destination. Perhaps early humans hiked up to Mount Pua and the unique flint mines in the Upper Galilee as part of a ceremonial, even spiritual journey.

In an exploratory dig at a random heap of rocks on Mount Pua, several deliberate stashes of processed flint tools were discovered at the bottom. There were thirteen tools in each stash. They were not stowed away for future use, because they were covered in piles of rubble and chippings. They were probably placed there as votives to the rock, a traditional gesture by prehistoric humans to the quarry for giving them its finest and to the cosmos for letting them use its rocks for their needs. Thirteen expertly chiseled tools were placed on the rock from which boulders of flint were mined, with the sincere intention of guaranteeing that the quarry would continue satisfying human needs forever.

Early humans did not only use natural resources for their own benefit. Their attitudes toward them were rooted in the same ontological worldview that characterized their view of elephants and other great mammals. They were all partners in a universe built of parallel worlds—that of humans, that of the animal kingdom, that of the rocks and mountains—and humans had to coexist with all these entities and respect them. In the Andes, which hosted the most significant stone-based cultures known to modern scholarship, rock quarries were perceived as the original inhabitants of the region. The stones were the landlords; the territory was registered in their name. They dressed them, fed them, and dedicated coca leaves to them. Human beings engaged in an intricate relationship with the rocks that served them.

***

Kathryn Weedman Arthur, an anthropologist from the University of South Florida who specializes in the study of stone technologies, is an excellent source of information about the lives of people who still maintain elements of the Stone Age lifestyle. Over the past twenty years, she has spent most of her time with the Gamo people in southern Ethiopia. She has her own hut there and is almost an organic part of the group. Just before international aviation was frozen because of the COVID-19 pandemic, we met her to hear what we, as members of Western civilization, were missing about the importance of stone.

Arthur, a cheerful woman who is enthusiastic about her subject matter, says that we are too rationalistic. Like many other archeologists, she was convinced at the outset of her work that anyone could develop a knack for flint-knapping. It might not be the simplest task in the world, like slicing bread, but it's definitely doable. All it takes is observation, watching how someone else does it right: grabbing tightly onto a stone, giving it a sharp whack, and hey presto, you've got a perfect blade. When she asked her regular fixer, a Gamo flint-knapper, to let her try her hand at knapping flint, he hesitated for one long moment, unsure how to respond to this bizarre request—she was not only a woman invading a male domain, but a white face who had just swooped in out of nowhere. Nevertheless, he was polite enough to give her a hunk of unprocessed flint. Arthur gripped the stone, raised her hand, and did everything that she was told to do. After a few minutes of strenuous and diligent masonry (at least in her view), she handed her work back to the local expert. This is how she describes his reaction: "The corner of his mouth twisted up in a half smile, and he furrowed his brow . . . With a look of exasperation, he said, *'t'unna,'* which means worthless. I was disappointed. 'Why?' I asked him. He smiled and scoffed, 'You should have learned from me.'"

In the twenty years after this incident, that's exactly what Arthur did. She learned that a skilled flint-knapper "must embody the correct status, practices, and reverence of the nonhuman world."

"Reverence of the nonhuman world" is a concept that requires explanation. This is one of the first things that Arthur does for readers of her book *The Lives of Stone Tools*, an intimate and engrossing portrait of modern-day flint-knappers. "The Boreda Gamo indigenous religion *Etta Woga* is a unique African philosophy," she writes, "and prescribes that all matter, including stone, comes into being through a reproductive process; . . . that all beings are gendered; and that all demonstrate a change in their status throughout their respective life cycles . . . Stones, river water, and rainbows . . . have power, tendency, and agency; . . . they are vital beings. Knappable stone begins life through the interaction of male rains penetrating the female womb of the earth . . . Knappable stones are male . . . [They] are circumcised through knapping and become male hidescraper youths shedding their wasteful material."

41

This is astonishing, especially after everything we thought we knew about prehistoric stone masonry. So maybe the abundant flint rubble scattered around Mount Pua, or at least some of it, was basically leftover "foreskins." Part of the process of circumcising the stone and its masons.

We met Arthur on a Friday afternoon at a popular bar in central Tel Aviv. It was near the end of winter in early 2020, and the place was brimming with youthful joy, relatively cheap alcohol, and excellent food. Nobody could have imagined that in a week this would all come to an abrupt end, we would start wearing masks, and this bar's regular patrons would have to save it (and others) with crowd-funding campaigns. Waiting for another round of drinks, Arthur explained that the groups with whom she had shared her professional life had beliefs that determined not just the status and life story of chiseled stones but of the people who did the chiseling. "Young flint-knappers experience birth, adolescence, adulthood, and death much like stone itself," she explains.

Truth be told, the importance of stone is not entirely alien to the modern Western mind. We carefully select headstones for our loved ones and make marble or granite memorials to commemorate (generally tragic) events in our national histories. We are all enthralled by stunning rocky landscapes and decorate our desks or bookshelves with special pebbles we pick up on hikes. In New Hampshire, there was a big rock that locals and tourists affectionately called the "Old Man of the Mountain" and attached human qualities to. Poems and stories have been written about it, and its image appeared on vehicle license plates. Unfortunately, the Old Man of the Mountain was destroyed in a rockslide in 2003. The way the governor of New Hampshire spoke of it, it was as if a close relative had died. It's not quite the same as shared coca leaf-chewing sessions with the rocks, as in the Andes, but it's not far off.

The prehistoric stonecutters bequeathed us not only flint and limestone rubble, but also a revolutionary approach to the inanimate natural world: the belief that it exists to serve us;

that it can be exploited for the benefit of humans; that it can be carved, dug, mined, broken, shattered, and smashed. They believed that there was no choice, and that it was impossible to move, to make any progress, without a good quarry. We forgot the respectful part of this equation long ago and have honed the exploitative part into an art form.

"The biggest risk to the cultural and environmental conservation of the rainforest might come from the subsoil. There is no greater danger than mining to the ecological integrity of Colombian Amazonia," wrote the popular Colombian novelist Héctor Abad when he returned from a trip into the depths of his own country's jungles, an area on the fault line between accelerated development and indigenous groups trying to protect their heritage and unique way of life. Abad targeted his criticism at a specific quarter: "With the defeat or retreat of the guerrillas, with the drug traffickers' disappointment, with the arrival of less corrupt and more efficient governments, a new type of persistent visitor has appeared in these frontier territories: geologists." The quarries, rocks, minerals, and high-quality stone that were once the sacred reserve of those who lived in the jungles and mountains had become an irresistible bounty for businesspeople and international consortia, driven by unsentimental cost–benefit calculations.

Modern quarries are perpetual sources of air pollution, unwanted noise, and constant damage to the natural terrain. There are over fifty major quarries in Israel, producing nearly 100 million tons a year. Up in the Andes, there are many times more quarries. The biggest quarry in the world, Thornton Quarry in Illinois, is 2.5km (1.5mi) wide and some 150m (500ft) deep. Thornton Quarry, like many others, is still mined for rock with great force. But nobody makes sacrificial offerings to the stone, and obviously nobody says "thank you" to it.

A contemporary stone knapper from Ethiopia

CHAPTER 4
LIGHT MY FIRE

400,000–200,000 years ago

From Qesem Cave in Israel to Ventura County, California

**When did early humans start using fire? How did
teeth lead to the discovery of a new human lineage?
Why should you be wary of raw meat diets?
And why is it so important to share?**

In the central square at the entrance to Kafr Qassem, an Arab
village in Israel, stands a large memorial. It's a narrow, inverted
pyramid, covered in slabs of black marble, with a datestone
at the top marking the year of the massacre committed here:
1956. Forty-six individuals—among them women, the elderly,
and children—were shot for violating a curfew order that they
knew nothing about. The perpetrators of this crime were tried;
the president of the State of Israel expressed condolences, after
a long delay; and still, no mention of or visit to Kafr Qassem,
which has long since become just another town in Israel, can
sidestep this tragic event. Not even after more than sixty years,
not even when telling a story that began tens or even hundreds
of thousands of years earlier. The massacre keeps the present
highly charged and wafts above you, even if you are only
searching for the long and distant past.

The streets of Kafr Qassem are clean, and the parking spaces
are marked out. The entrance to the town is full of hardware
stores, shops selling building materials, and "wholesalers"
selling fruit and vegetables at prices that are just as marked up
as anywhere else. At the top of the hill, in the ancient part of

this Arab town, is a maze of picturesque alleyways that are often used as the backdrop for movies set in places far away and many years ago. It could be a Moroccan alley or a street in an Oriental epic set in the mid-nineteenth century.

A few hundred meters beyond the southeastern edge of Kafr Qassem, just behind the football stadium, runs Highway 5, a strip of asphalt comfortably and directly connecting the Greater Tel Aviv area to the heart of the West Bank. When the road was inaugurated in the late 1980s, it caused uproar in Israel. Left-wing activists gate-crashed the festive ceremony and tried to disrupt it. The newspapers dubbed the road the "Cross-Nation Highway," because of how divisive it was. This was a long time ago—or in terms of the events described in this book, about a second ago.

When Highway 5 was expanded in 2000, speleologist Amos Frumkin left his home in the Samarian Hills to conclude his study of a stalactite cave abutting a new-and-improved junction. He parked his Peugeot pick-up truck next to the roadwork diggers and walked over to the cave that he had been studying for a while. On his way, he suddenly noticed a deep and fresh fissure in the earth. It revealed what looked like the remains of another cave, whose ceiling had collapsed.

Underground caverns are not only the subject of much of Frumkin's academic research but also the scene of most of his professional life, if not his life in general. He founded and currently manages the Israel Cave Research Center, did his PhD on salt caves in the Judean Desert, and moved heaven and earth (both the bits above ground and those below it) to restore the title of "longest salt cave in the world" to one of these caves, after a faulty measurement stripped it of its glory. (Someone who once crawled along the route marked out by a winding cord that Frumkin had stretched through the narrow passageways in a dark cave recalls that after half an hour, before even reaching the mid-point of the cave, he was begging to go back to the surface. But there was no going back.) Frumkin lowered himself deeper, grasping the tip of the cord that if released, would leave him stuck in the bowels of this cave forever.

In short, who knows what would have happened if someone else had parked his pick-up truck near the heavy machinery working on the Highway 5 expansion, or if this Hebrew University geography professor had found another parking spot that day? But Frumkin was the man on the scene, and when he peeked into the collapsed cave, he saw at once that it contained buried treasure.

The cave expert called the Antiquities Authority and reported his discovery, but he also picked up the phone to the duo from Mount Pua in the previous chapter: Avi Gopher and Ran Barkai. They both worked at Tel Aviv University's Archeology Department, at the far end of Highway 5. This phone call changed the course of scholarship (and the course of the highway) forever. If the contractor had known what a mess he was getting himself into, he'd have probably done everything he could to stop Frumkin from peeking at what his diggers had unearthed just a day or two earlier. But it was too late, the academics were on their way, and when they saw what Frumkin had described, the contractor would have to find reserves of patience—something earthwork professionals are not usually blessed with. This episode would cost him and the public works department dearly because Israeli law generously requires the costs of rescue digs to be borne by the contractor in charge. Every construction or development budget in Israel has a line for unexpected costs in case archeological treasures are discovered under the site of new houses or roads.

When Frumkin called, Gopher and Barkai were focused mainly on the Neolithic era: some 15,000 years ago, hundreds of thousands of years after the Paleolithic. As they walked between the rocky landscape overlooking Highway 5, they understood immediately that their future—and not just the contractor's—was about to change forever. Deep inside the exposed rock was a huge, practically inconceivable quantity of flint tools and animal bones, which they could discern even before grabbing a single shovel or sieve to work through the piles of dirt. Even a second- or third-year archeology college student could have told you that these were blades and scrapers: the characteristic cutting tools of the culture that flourished some 400,000 years ago. A totally different period from Gopher and Barkai's field of expertise. Different—but pregnant with possibility and mystery.

***

"It is not the strongest of the species that survives, nor the most intelligent that survives. It is the one that is most adaptable to change," Charles Darwin, the father of the theory of evolution, is popularly misquoted as saying—but it's true. Human beings are certainly adaptable to change. After hundreds of thousands of years of blessed technological conservatism and migration along safe and familiar routes, they pivoted and broadened their horizons. The humans we met in the Jordan Valley—the elephant-hunters at Daughters of Jacob's Bridge and the flint-knappers in the mountains of the Galilee—underwent a transformation.

Hundreds of thousands of years ago, in the rolling hills around Kafr Qassem, roamed wild horses and wild boars (which are genetically different from those we know today), wild asses, and aurochs that grew up to 3m (10ft) long and over 2m (7ft) tall. In the long, low valley where cars now drive, herds of nimble and elusive fallow deer once frolicked. All these species, and especially the fallow deer, were part of the world of the humans who lived there. In fact, they might have been the main reason why humans showed up there in the first place. Humans migrated in pursuit of herds of animals, recognized their footprints, and maybe even gave them names to mark out the old and the young, the quick and the slow, the lean and those bursting with all-important fat. The Sami people, modern-day deer-hunters in northern Norway, have 600 words to describe deer in different situations but mostly to describe seasonal fluctuations in their fat content. The Inuit in northern Canada have over twenty words to describe reindeer, each describing a distinct physiological state. It would not be a stretch of the imagination to assume that people living in a totally different era also had different terms to distinguish bony fallow deer from the caloric bonanzas on legs.

The proportion of an animal's fat content is important. Critical. Hunters do not leave their rock shelters to wear themselves down hunting rice cakes or emaciated fallow deer. It's doubtful whether the energy required for the chase could justify the effort. Hunting is a deliberate, planned enterprise, based on much more of a cost–benefit analysis than modern-day breadwinners are familiar with. This was especially true across the Levant 400,000 years ago, when an ecological catastrophe and/or overhunting by humans pulled their most popular supplies of fat off the shelves: elephants.

In the twenty-first century, we fret about the disappearance of other animal species and feel sad whenever a heartless hunter kills an elephant or a rhinoceros to sell its tusks or horn. There are also protesters and activists who board speedboats to try to stop whale-hunters. Pamela Anderson, of *Baywatch* fame, was shown in a televised documentary locking horns with fishermen in the Faroe Islands, trying to obstruct their traditional hunt. It definitely helped the documentary's ratings. We feel sincerely concerned about dwindling elephant and whale populations, but for prehistoric humans, extinction was a genuine earthquake. It upended their world. Elephants were not wiped out overnight: this was a gradual process, but the material and mental ramifications were nevertheless enormous.

It didn't happen only in the Levant, or only 400,000 years ago. When woolly mammoths disappeared in the Arctic Siberia 15,000 years ago (probably for reasons similar to those for the disappearance of elephants in the Levant), the people who lived on the band of ice between Asia and North America had to adapt in far-reaching ways. Not because they had nothing to hunt or eat (they did), but because they were suddenly missing the basic resources for making hunting tools. The raw materials that they had used were no longer available.

In the barren wastelands of the north, the huge bones and tusks of woolly mammoths were an essential natural resource—just like flint boulders were for those who made stone tools in areas closer to the Levant. After the peoples of Siberia had finished using the mammoth skeletons they found in the ice even centuries after these great beasts were driven extinct, and they were left without their familiar hard materials, they had to perform a volte-face and reinvent themselves. New tool-manufacturing technologies emerged in the Arctic; hunting methods evolved; and people started following herds of bison as they migrated south to a new continent. And all (or most) of this was because of the disappearance of the mammoths.

There are many other diverse examples of the impact of the disappearance of animals on prehistoric humans: key terms in the Māori language in New Zealand were influenced by the extinction of the moa, an enormous bird; the Thule people in northern Canada migrated into unknown lands at the end of the first millennium after the dwindling of the bowhead whale population in nearby bays; transportation corridors in the African savanna were erased as fewer and fewer elephants roamed there. It is hard to overstate the importance of the connection between animals and hunter-gatherers, past and present.

Elephants are not the only animals to have disappeared from the Levant. *Homo erectus*, who ruled the roost for hundreds of thousands of years, are also nowhere to be seen. They didn't quite "disappear"—that's not the right verb to explain what happened—but they are no longer with us. "Changed" would be a more suitable and scientific term, or perhaps "transformed," or "became a different kind of human in an evolutionary process that lasted hundreds of thousands of years." In Europe, we shall meet them again in the form of Neanderthals; and in Africa, a different process occurred, resulting in modern humans making their appearance. This also took hundreds of thousands of years, with so many question marks along the way. And the answers or explanations for at least some of them were buried under the heaps of dirt and rock that had collapsed into the cave opening on the shoulder of Highway 5 in modern-day Israel.

All that was left to do was to dig.

***

Inspectors from the Israel Antiquities Authority blocked the continuation of the development works, Barkai and Gopher won the tender to conduct exploratory digs at the cave, and the frustrated contractor was left pulling his hair out. At one point, he was willing to offer over $1 million to be guaranteed that the process would be quick—one excavation season and that's that—and that his bulldozers could soon return to action. The archeologists resisted the temptation. They wanted to work at their own pace, to check every inch by the book. One season went by, and the next, and the next. They gave the cave a suitable name: *Qesem*, meaning "magic" in Hebrew.

The world's top archeologists stood by these two academics and explained that it's not every day that such a special site gets discovered. The collapse of the cave roof tens of thousands of years ago had trapped the past underground, promising the preservation of the treasures lurking within. The Antiquities Authority backed up the researchers and it took nothing less than the intervention of the Israeli Prime Minister's Office to reach what always lies at the end of such headaches: a compromise. The highway was moved by a few dozen meters, the archeologists "scarified" part of the site, the contractor built a new roof to preserve the cave, and the prime minister moved on to dealing with other problems. No fewer than sixteen excavation seasons have come and gone since then. Their findings are tantalizing.

There are no elephant remains in Qesem Cave. Their unequivocal absence is no less important to science than everything that *was* discovered. In the professional jargon, we say that the absence of evidence is also evidence. Elephant remains have been found at many known sites from before this period, all from over 400,000 years ago. Jordi Rosell and Ruth Blasco, a pair of archeozoologists from Spain (or Catalonia, more accurately, to respect the nationalist fervor of at least one of them), spent many weeks at Qesem Cave. They sifted through bones, scanned them with electron microscopes, carefully inspected them one by one—and found no trace of any elephants. They did find the bones of many other animals that we have already mentioned: fallow deer, wild asses, wild pigs, aurochs, horses, and even tortoises, which must have been eaten as hors d'oeuvres before the main course. They found incision marks on the fallow deer bones, proof that the animals had been expertly carved up and maybe even distributed in an orderly fashion within the group. They looked much like the marks that a neighborhood butcher might leave on a bone, and nothing like the cuts that might have been caused by other predators.

The question of the distribution of meat was much more significant: sharing is one of the hallmarks of modern-day indigenous societies. The sharing of property, belongings, land, and food is the bread and butter of their existence and approach to life. They are especially judicious about applying this approach to the distribution of hunting spoils. Everyone is entitled to their share, irrespective of their role in the hunt and regardless of who tracked down the fallow deer or who scored the fatal hit with an arrow.

The archeological record confirms that this pattern of behavior was also prevalent in the past. Sometimes hunt leaders or successful archers were given their pick of the spoils as soon as they killed a deer, but when it came to chopping up the carcass at home, everyone was equal. This was a highly successful survival strategy. A prehistoric mechanism of mutual responsibility.

Qesem Cave mostly welcomed deliveries of fallow deer heads and front and back legs for distribution. They were a major part of the diet of the people who lived there. They ate huge quantities of fallow deer and tried to focus on the adults, which had the greatest fat reserves. Fallow deer—like wild asses, gazelles, and other ungulates—are medium-sized, quick on their feet, and move in large groups. Almost the total opposite of proboscideans (elephants and mammoths), which are huge, relatively slow, and wander alone or in small families.

It is not easy to pivot from being expert elephant-hunters to chasing fallow deer. It is, like they say in sports, a totally different ball game. To get anywhere near the caloric payload a single elephant once provided, prehistoric humans had to catch at least eighty fallow deer. They had to be more agile than in the past, quicker but not necessarily as strong. Most importantly, they had to work in groups, to collaborate. On one hill stood those who scouted the deer; on another stood those who chased them; and in the valley in between were their comrades who set up obstacles for their prey. They developed a social dynamic that was unlikely to have existed previously.

Humans' hunting and cutting tools also evolved. The hand axe, the handy gizmo that had proven its usefulness for over one million years, lost its primacy to sharp flint blades and scrapers, which were efficient for skinning the edible meat of smaller animals. Hand axes were rare finds at Qesem Cave, and the few that were found there probably came from older sites and were not made there. They too, like elephants, also disappeared from the landscape, and the disappearance of one was apparently linked to the disappearance of the other. Changes in hunting practices led to changes in hunting and meat-carving technologies and methods. But that's not the whole picture. Because the people who lived in Qesem Cave did not just *eat* meat—they barbecued it.

***

The story of prehistoric humans' relationship with fire is complicated and academically contested. Just say the word "fire" at a conference of prehistorians and you'll whip up the flames yourself. When did humans first start using fire? Where? How? Was it an accident? Intentional? The mastery of fire is critical to understanding humanity's development, and Darwin considered it an even more significant step than the invention of tools, second in importance only to the invention of language.

Unlike all other animals, humans struggle to extract caloric value from uncooked food. With all due respect to trendy raw food diets, in order to survive and develop we prefer to consume cooked food, like our distant ancestors. Contemporary research shows that urban foodies on fashionable raw food diets suffer from chronic energy deficiencies. These studies back up an extreme position in the argument over the history (or prehistory) of the use of fire, which takes the story back nearly two million years. This theory is not based on evidence of the use of fire (almost no such evidence exists, and one of the only and earliest traces discovered to date is from Daughters of Jacob's Bridge, from 750,000 years ago), but on the conditions and reasons for anatomical changes in early humans.

Richard Wrangham, from the Human Evolutionary Biology Department at Harvard University, wrote a book whose title encapsulates his position: *Catching Fire: How Cooking Made Us Human*. He argues that the caloric "profit" that humans gained from eating grilled or cooked food—i.e. the energy they saved from not having to chew and digest raw meat—allowed the human brain to grow and individuals (especially women) to gain body mass. Meanwhile, the human jaw's molar count fell, and humans started to become slightly less hairy—with campfires to warm them, they no longer needed fur from head to toe. According to this theory, it was thanks to fire that we were able to sleep peacefully on the earth, protected from the cold and predators. A long and comfortable night's sleep, as every parent knows, is a necessary condition for physical growth. Two million years ago, it was thanks to fire that *Homo erectus* children were able to fall asleep on the warm soil.

Opposing Wrangham are those who believe that it is impossible to speak of the conscious and continued use of fire until around 40,000 years ago. This polar opposite opinion is based on the absence of charred remains and traces of campfires at several of the caves that served Neanderthals in western Europe. This absence points to a lack of control over fire, for if they had controlled fire, they would have certainly used it for their benefit. Fire is a dominant and multi-purpose element of hunter-gatherer societies. It is used for extracting grease from bones, making tools, defense, forest clearance for habitation, heating, and of course cooking. It's inconceivable that people who knew how to keep fires going willingly gave up on this option, just for the fun of it. According to this theory, Neanderthals only used fire in random and haphazard ways and settled the chilly and often frozen continent of Europe without the help of regular fires.

Somewhere in the middle, between one theory and another, lies Qesem Cave. It's not two million years old, and certainly not 40,000 years old, but definitely 400,000 years old. Indeed, Qesem Cave was found to contain evidence of the earliest known continued and deliberate use of fire for grilling meat: evidence of campfires in the inner parts of the cave, organized human activity around these points, blades and other flint tools forged in the fire, and a range of animal bones that had once been on a Palaeolithic barbecue.

The evidence of the continued use of fire at Qesem Cave excited the imagination of many scholars, was unpacked in reams of scientific papers, and was debated (not without resistance and forceful counterarguments) at high-level international conferences. It provided exactly what was missing from a theory developed by an independent scholar by the name of Chaim Chayat.

Chayat is self-taught and lacks an academic (or even secondary school) education. He is a car mechanic by trade, a part-time painter and copywriter who likes to dream and ride his big old motorbike. He dedicated ten years of his life to deciphering the essence of time, and then he stumbled on the subject of fire at Qesem Cave. Chayat published an ambitious non-fiction book titled *Nothingness, Time, and the Missing Link*, and much of his thesis is based on what he calls the "sheltering of fire." Hayat argues that the people who had the job of watching over the fire in the caves developed a routine. This was something that had not previously existed: work, a daily schedule, regularity. The routine of stoking the campfire gave time a new meaning, and people who had previously been in permanent motion switched gears. To keep their embers burning, they needed a conceptual time clock.

Chayat's argument is neat and original, even if it gets tangled in places because of problems of style and phrasing on the part of a man who has much more experience fixing car engines than writing scientific literature. In any case, it is a shame that fewer than ten people bought the book and that even fewer read the whole thing. But Chayat did not despair, and he's using his unemployment benefits to finance the writing of a follow-up book. He's not short on time.

***

In Qesem Cave (and probably also in similar caves that have not yet been discovered by errant tractors or bulldozers), people obviously did much more than hold barbeque parties. The flint tools discovered in the cave are stored in rows of drawers in the prehistory laboratory at Tel Aviv University. The tools that did not make it into these drawers got stashed into cardboard boxes stacked on top of each other in the corridors, blocking access to the water cooler and biscuit tin. It is always exciting to see tools hundreds of thousands of years old, even if you're not the biggest fan of prehistoric archeology. You hold a flint blade between your fingers and it feels like a postcard from the distant past. Very distant, but very human. It was made by thinking humans, humans who were capable of making plans.

The people who lived in Qesem Cave chiseled their flint tools with precision and care. Like the earlier flint-knappers at Mount Pua, here too it seems that practical technological knowledge was passed from father to son, from generation to generation. These prehistoric cave-dwellers were even using environmentally friendly and recycled materials instead of throwing them in the bin, or whatever they called landfill sites back then. Gopher and Barkai's talented students identified fragments of tools that had become dulled or broken and were turned into smaller but still useful knives. This was the earliest known evidence of the recycling of raw materials that were not always available, and even if they were, wastefulness is a modern vice. Hunter-gatherers, even today and certainly in the past, were for the most part calculating and frugal characters.

During the tenth excavation season at the cave, Rosell and Blasco, the archeozoological duo from Spain, stumbled upon an unidentified bone. It didn't belong to a fallow deer, nor even to an auroch or a wild boar. Neither academic had ever felt left out of the action: when they were not at Qesem Cave, they were busy conducting comparative studies on how black bears shattered bones up in the Pyrenees and digging deep into the Atapuerca Caves in Spain. But they were enchanted by this Levantine cave, and especially by this unusual and unfamiliar bone. After running it through repeated laboratory tests, they discovered that it was part of the wing of a swan: not one of the most common birds in these parts at that period, and definitely not one found every day at prehistoric sites. Nevertheless, at least one swan wing had made its way to Qesem Cave. The people who lived there probably were not after the swan's lean meat, but its breathtaking plumage. The incision marks on the wing bone clearly show that its feathers had been carefully removed.

In their academic imagination, Rosell and Blasco associated the feathers with some sort of ritual activity that took place in Qesem Cave hundreds of thousands of years ago. If they are correct, this would be the earliest archeological proof in the world of such activity. In later periods, and until recently, indigenous groups used to beautify themselves with feathers, weaving them into their hair or into their flint tools. Native Americans in

Westerns offer a familiar example of such decorations. At face value, decorations are decorations. Something aesthetic, no matter what period you're living in. But the feathers of swans, vultures, or any other majestic bird might have had a deeper level of meaning: a desire to *be like the birds* and soar to the heavens. This is a bold possibility, taking such phenomena much further back than usual in academic research, but after so many seasons among the intangible spirit and tangible remains of the inhabitants of Qesem Cave, anything seems possible.

***

No skull or skeleton belonging to the cave's inhabitants has been found—not even a prehistoric human rib or femur. But teeth have, thirteen teeth from different individuals, mostly under the age of twenty, who lived in Qesem Cave 300,000–400,000 years ago. Despite their minuscule size, teeth are among the archeological findings that inspire the greatest joy. They allow us to work out their former owners' exact age and help us understand an individual's biological development at any given site. Our teeth, from the moment they erupt, are affected by changes in our lifestyles and environment. They are treasure troves of information: What have you eaten? How did you chew it? Did you brush your teeth? Did you use dental floss? And what can I see here, *is that a stuck piece of corn?*

Rachel Sarig, an orthodontist who specializes in teeth straightening, is also a dental anthropologist. She is a regular feature on lists of "most promising young people" in Israel, and her lectures are delivered to packed houses. She begins them with a piece of trivia that surprises everyone: the most common human disease in the world throughout history is tooth decay. That's enough to grab everyone's attention and make them rush to the dental hygienist as soon as they get out the door. Sarig joined the researchers at Qesem Cave, and she concludes that the teeth discovered there do not match those of *Homo erectus*. They are something else, slightly different. They bear a certain, partial resemblance to Neanderthal teeth, and they look much more like the teeth of the humans who lived only 100,000 years ago in caves on Mount Carmel and near Nazareth.

Sarig's dental findings and biting conclusions bolstered the researchers' impressions of the inhabitants of Qesem Cave. They were human beings from a new human lineage. Not *Homo erectus*, but not quite *Homo sapiens* or Neanderthals either. They were an interim species, another link in a tangled chain that did not follow a straightforward course. The disappearance of elephants was apparently an important trigger for humanity's evolutionary adaptation: the brains of the human inhabitants of Qesem Cave were probably bigger than those of *Homo erectus*, their legs probably got longer, and their bodies were lighter. They were also faster, more social, and more skilled with new technologies.

In the Samarian Hills once lived humans who knew how to use fire, loved eating grilled meat, made new kinds of tools, and kept circling back to the same point. To their cave: Qesem Cave.

***

The sun that beat down on us at this Paleolithic cave begins to set slowly over the coastal plain and the skyscrapers of Tel Aviv. Airplanes loop around above our heads before descending into the international airport. On the hill, at the top of the mosque, the muezzin calls the faithful to prayer. An English author, who plans to write a book about Qesem Cave, climbs onto the adjacent hill and jots down in his notepad that the actress Gal Gadot grew up in a nearby city. Each has his own world of associations. The traffic flows on Highway 5 as people return from work, minutes away from putting their keys on the table, asking what's for dinner, and catching up on the news.

Far from here, the world is on fire. From California to India, Angola to Australia, hundreds of thousands of acres are going up in flames, people are fleeing their homes, and millions of animals are being annihilated. In Ventura and Riverside counties in southern California, wildfires have eliminated over 43km² (17mi²) of forests, including one of the biggest reserves of beautiful Joshua trees. In Brazil, the fires in the Amazon rainforest are almost impossible to monitor. These are just a few examples from daily news reports during the writing of this book.

Stephen Pyne, an environmental historian and the author of *Fire: A Brief History*, proposes calling the modern era the "Age of Fire," the period in which fires became regular parts of the landscape, like frozen ice did in the past. Pyne notes that besides open forest fires, we are also burning coal, petroleum, and gas on a hidden but colossal scale. By forging a pact with fire to survive, we let it thrive and get totally out of control. Like stone quarries, and probably so much more, what looked like an efficient and necessary invention tens or hundreds of thousands of years ago has snowballed into a tangible threat. Humans and fire—which might have first been domesticated in Qesem Cave—are fundamentally transforming our planet. And not necessarily for the better.

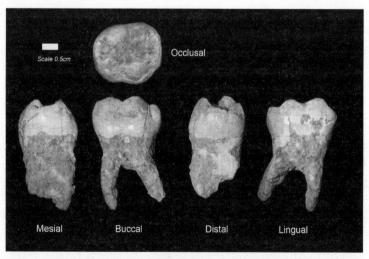

Human tooth unearthed at Qesem Cave and dated to approximately 400,000 years ago

CHAPTER 5

GOOD NEIGHBORS

100,000–40,000 years ago

**From the Mount Carmel Caves in Israel to
Gorham's Cave in Gibraltar**

**Why should one not believe the Neanderthals' bad
reputation? What relations did they have with
Homo sapiens? Where was the last place Neanderthals
lived? And why did they disappear while we remained?**

In the winter of 1928, reports appeared in the Hebrew press
in Mandatory Palestine about plans to build a port in the Bay
of Haifa. The British Empire was looking for a harbor for its
celebrated merchant navy to dock at on its way to the East,
and Haifa's natural bay, which had functioned as a commercial
port back in Crusader times, was a natural choice. The Zionist
visionary Theodor Herzl hoped that this would be the maritime
gateway of the future Jewish state.

These reports turned into reality a few months later, and the
task of planning and building the Port of Haifa fell to Lords
Rendel, Palmer, and Tritton of the engineering firm that bore
their name, one of the most highly regarded and experienced
companies in the field. To build a port of the magnitude of the
one planned for Haifa, the planners first had to locate high-
quality stone quarries for the materials. The importance of
stone as a building block of human existence had only grown
over the past 2.5 million years; to mix metaphors, it also oiled
the wheels of progress. Two sites were identified as potential
candidates: the first was next to a Crusader fortress south of

Haifa; the second was in Wadi el-Mughara (Nahal Me'arot) on the western slopes of Mount Carmel. Both sites were sufficiently close to the Bay of Haifa and full of fine limestone reserves.

Shortly after the stone quarries were selected, Naim Makhouly, an inspector in the Mandatory Department of Antiquities, was asked to investigate whether there were any significant archeological sites in Wadi el-Mughara. The British were aware of Palestine's rich prehistoric past, and archeological preservation was one of their governing goals. Research in this area was still in its infancy, but an initial probe had already revealed a fascinating snapshot from the distant past: the skull of "Galilee Man," discovered by Francis Turville-Petre (or rather, his dog) in Wadi Amud, and the discoveries by Dorothy Garrod. She excavated the Shuqba Cave in Wadi en-Natuf, northeast of Lydda, and identified a unique culture that existed 15,000–12,000 years ago and came to be known as "Natufian" culture. We shall reach this stage in our human journey in Chapter 7.

Makhouly set out from his offices in Acre on donkeyback. After an eight-and-a-half-hour ride (this must have been an especially stubborn donkey), he reached his destination. At the entrance to Wadi el-Mughara were three familiar caves: Tabun (literally "oven," named for the shape of its interior) and considered the smallest and least important; Jamal ("Camel"); and El-Wad ("Stream"). The latter cave, perhaps because of its depth, twisting structure, and creepy acoustics, was the subject of local fables and superstitions about demons from the distant past. Sir Laurence Oliphant, a British Christian mystic and ardent Zionist who lived in a Druze village in the Carmel mountains in the nineteenth century, described in his memoirs how he had crawled into the bowels of the cave in search of demons and had found only legions of bats. There was also a fourth cave, the Es-Skhul ("Kid") Cave, but this did not even appear on the antiquities inspector's to-do list.

Makhouly conducted a cursory investigation of the three caves, but as soon as he started, he got the feeling that they contained something of value beyond bats and ghosts. In his memoirs, he wrote that these were large natural caves containing many objects made by prehistoric humans. The objects were flint tools in a range of sizes, which were found scattered on the ground. Usually when such discoveries are made above the surface, one can assume that many more like them are hiding underground.

Makhouly handed his findings to his boss, Ernest Richmond, the director of the Mandatory Antiquities Department and a bitter foe of the Zionist enterprise. He was a fervent pro-Arabist, an associate and advisor of Haj Amin al-Husseini, the anti-semitic mufti of Jerusalem. If it had been up to Richmond, these caves would have long been part of an independent Palestinian Arab state. The antiquities director lacked the power to make this dream come true, but he certainly had the authority to block approval for quarrying at Wadi el-Mughara.

Back at the offices of Rendel, Palmer & Tritton in London, the engineers behind the Port of Haifa thought that they were losing their minds. They already had diggers and cranes on their way to a hugely important maritime project, and suddenly a random bureaucrat was giving them nonsense about an archeological site that might not contain anything after all. They held meetings with government ministries, exchanged correspondence between London and Jerusalem (most of the letters were polite, some only superficially so), and aired their grievances and reservations. Precious time was lost, and after all this and countless cups of tea and trays of biscuits, it was decided to suspend quarrying operations until an organized exploratory dig could go ahead. But then it turned out that officials in London had thought that the fuss was about a Crusader fortress, not the Wadi el-Mughara caves. Caves? What caves, for goodness' sake?

This set off another round of correspondence and meetings until it was decided to put the matter to rest once and for all and start building the Port of Haifa. The engineering company allocated £150 for the exploratory dig, and the money was transferred to the Antiquities Department along with a letter clarifying that at the end of the excavations, it would be proper to remove the caves from the list of protected sites under antiquities laws, unless something of importance were found. Nobody expected anything of the sort to be discovered.

Turville-Petre and Garrod, Mandatory Palestine's senior prehistorians, were preoccupied at the time with an excavation in southern Kurdistan, hundreds of miles from the caves on Mount Carmel. The task fell to the numismatist Charles Lambert—an expert in ancient coins. Not exactly the most qualified person to lead prehistoric excavations, but the only one available at the Antiquities Department. To Lambert's credit, he was diligent and aware of the time pressure. In early November 1928, he set up a tent encampment at the entrance to the site and immediately set about exploring the El-Wad Cave. He reported on the abundance of flint fragments that Makhouly had spotted on the ground, but he dug over a meter into the ground and found many stone tools that looked just like those that Garrod had found and classified as belonging to Natufian culture. Lambert had not visited Garrod's excavations, but he had read everything he could to find his way around a period without coins or money. He kept digging and reported and photographed the plethora of stone tools that he unearthed in the upper strata of the El-Wad Cave.

It was an especially rainy winter—water leaked through the top of the team's tents, and one of Lambert's assistants decided to climb up to the Tabun Cave to see whether it might provide alternative shelter. Two and a half steps in, the assistant understood that the cave was much bigger than previously thought, and that beyond the entrance was a huge cavern with a natural shaft. To his astonishment, at the base of the shaft he found a cache of hand axes: the trademark invention of the Acheulean culture, hundreds of thousands of years before their time. The option of sleeping in the caves fell off the agenda.

One month after the exploratory digs began, Lambert came across a blackened bone that had been polished and worked into an animal head. It would come to be considered one of the earliest artworks in the Levant and undoubtedly one of the most beautiful findings at the site. This item was the handle of a sickle for crop harvesting, fashioned by a craftsman into the shape of a gazelle. A few days later, the archeologists found a prehistoric human skeleton, buried on the terrace outside the El-Wad Cave. Other skeletons would soon be unearthed nearby. They all belonged to *Homo sapiens*: modern humans. Some were found lying next to burial offerings, such as beads and shells.

By now, one thing was clear to everyone: the Port of Haifa would need to find a quarry elsewhere. The port's planners received a letter informing them that the caves had proven to be far more important than originally thought, and in fact one of the most promising prehistoric sites ever discovered. Something else was beyond doubt: these excavations had to be taken over by someone with much more training and experience in the field of prehistory. The choice was simple: Dorothy Garrod.

Garrod was born into the British intellectual aristocracy. Her father, Sir Archibald Garrod, was a professor of medicine at the University of Oxford and is considered the founding father of biochemical genetics; her grandfather, Sir Alfred Garrod, was one of Queen Victoria's favorite physicians and an expert in rheumatic diseases. Dorothy Garrod had little choice but to excel, and that's exactly what she did, only with a rebellious twist in her choice of subject—archeology instead of medicine.

In the early twentieth century, archeology was considered more of a hobby than a scientific discipline. Young students entered the field as a last chance or convenient fallback option, after failing to find their place in more prestigious faculties, such as medicine or law. They were warned that they could not expect a glittering career, and certainly not an income. In the latter respect, at least, not much has changed. Garrod was unimpressed by conventional wisdom and decided to blaze her own path in a highly unconventional direction, certainly for women.

She reached Wadi el-Mughara with an all-female team: Harriet Allyn and Martha Hackett from the American School of Archeology in Jerusalem, Elinor Ewbank from Oxford, and Mary Kitson Clark from Cambridge. They were all consummate professionals. They were joined by many Arab women from nearby villages, working as day laborers in the exhausting digging operation.

Despite having afternoon tea every day at 5pm and downing a bottle of expensive sherry every evening, the women didn't find conditions at the camp easy, to put it mildly. Heat, humidity, and dust storms make regular appearances in the excavation team's diaries. "There were forecasts for fragments of cloud, an earthquake, and the end of the world," wrote one member. "Mud, rubbish, and torn tents," wrote another, describing their surroundings. *Khamsin*, an especially intolerable form of Middle Eastern heatwave, also makes an appearance in their diaries, transliterating a word in the languages of both sets of locals, Jews and Arabs.

The tent encampment itself was exceptionally austere, if not downright miserable. It was lacking in running water but replete with furious assaults by flies during the day and mosquitoes at night. During the first excavation season, Kitson Clark was bitten and fell ill with ehrlichiosis, a tick-borne disease. Another member of the expedition was taken to a hospital in Haifa suffering from malaria. This was a grueling business, and Garrod ran the operation like a British officer in a war movie: with restraint, emotional distance, wry humor, and a silk pocket handkerchief. Besides the silk handkerchief, she had it all.

Thus began Garrod's life's work. Her six archeological seasons on Mount Carmel would make her an icon in her field and would establish the caves there as the basis of modern prehistoric research.

***

In the mid-nineteenth century, decades before Garrod set foot in the caves of Mount Carmel, archeologists in the Neander Valley in Germany found the fossilized remains of a human species that would come to be known as the Neanderthals. If anyone has a strong case for a defamation suit, not as an individual but as a whole human species, it's them. "Neanderthal" remains a powerful insult.

Erroneous scientific observations, deliberate bias, and limited knowledge, combined with Victorian conservatism and clericalism gave Neanderthals little hope of receiving a fair portrayal. Certainly not an accurate one. Neanderthals were said to be short, hairy, ugly, intellectually challenged, and more ape than human. Darwin had not yet published his theory of evolution, the Bible still offered the authoritative account of creation, and the idea that we were descended from apes was heresy. Let apes be apes, and let us be what we are: beautiful, straight-backed, and skilled. With no embarrassing relatives.

The Neanderthals were lumbered with this image for decades. Not just that, but also scholarly interpretations that were completely groundless and even downright false. Another Neanderthal skeleton, discovered in 1908 in the La Chapelle-aux-Saints Cave in France, only bolstered anti-Neanderthal prejudice. Marcellin Boule, a paleontologist from the National History Museum in Paris, convinced himself that this was the skeleton of a young and healthy person and therefore concluded that his species must have been short, hunchbacked, and deformed. This was in fact an old and sick Neanderthal man, but this fact was not appreciated until much later.

Boule, an influential academic, concluded that the Neanderthals were a tangential and insignificant offshoot in human evolution, and that was how they were treated for many years to come. It was assumed that Neanderthals were an earlier species than *Homo sapiens* and, given the progressive notion that we are the crowning glory of all creation and the reason for the world's existence, Neanderthals were obviously a less successful species. A failed experiment. The Neanderthals were classified alongside other extinct animal species, such as woolly mammoths and rhinoceroses. Primeval, almost mythological creatures that roamed Planet Earth in dark and scary times: the age of Neanderthals.

It was thought that Neanderthals were limited to western Europe, clumsy and vulnerable creatures who met their end when *Homo sapiens* marched out of Africa and pushed them into oblivion. In the racist and condescending Europe of the nineteenth and early twentieth centuries, it took little effort to preach to an audience that believed the world was divided into two: us and them, the superior species that survived, and the inferior species that was wiped out. Europe fancied itself the center of the world, and the Neanderthal story would soon serve to validate such evil philosophies as scientific racism. The Neanderthals' bitter fate seemed to provide an early example of how to deal with anyone who did not belong to the master race.

The information we have today paints an almost totally opposite picture. The Neanderthals lived for hundreds of thousands of years (from around 400,000 years ago till around 40,000 years ago) in a vast expanse between the Iberian Peninsula in the west and Siberia in the east. They survived long ice ages, adapted to difficult environmental conditions, became expert hunters, and were supported by a diverse economy. Their stone-tool production technology (known as the Levallois technique, named after the archeological site in a suburb of Paris where it was first classified) attests to exceptionally impressive planning and performance abilities. Although *Homo erectus* was the first to invent this method of stonemasonry, it was a marginal affair. The Neanderthals upgraded it into their commercial trademark.

Levallois was a tool-making technique more reminiscent of artistic sculpting than "industrial" flint-knapping. If the beauty of a hand axe is its symmetrical appearance, then the trick, even the genius, of the Levallois method lies in early planning. Having decided on the desired shape of the tool, Neanderthals crafted it out of chunks of rock using a wasteful chipping process. The final product was worth the effort. It was sharp as a razor, rock solid, and effective. These pointy objects were fashioned into spearheads and served the Neanderthals throughout their existence, allowing them to hunt huge animals such as mammoths and rhinoceroses from close range.

Neanderthals were no less skilled and effective a human species than us. They enjoyed a brain volume of 1.6l (2.8pt), compared with our own 1.4l (2.5pt) or slightly more. This is not necessarily proof of an intellectual advantage, but it is definitely not proof of the superiority of modern humans.

If you met a Neanderthal in the street wearing a suit and tie, you would probably notice that he looked slightly different from us, just as Europeans notice that Asian tourists look different, and vice versa. Neanderthals were slightly shorter than the average modern human, had large, broad noses (perhaps this helped them to adapt to the cold and dryness by gradually heating the air that they breathed), and lacked our pronounced chins. A Neanderthal in a suit and tie might be able to blend into a crowd by wearing a hat, but this would disguise a fundamentally differently shaped skull. It was elongated and relatively flat, compared to modern humans' round heads. At the back was a kind of small bump, like the shape formed by tying one's hair in a bun.

The Neanderthals were much more muscular and toned than us. Their teeth were bigger and stronger, and they used them not just to bite and chew food but also to grab and pull things when their hands were busy. Their brow lines were more pronounced and created a ridge above their eyes. In this sense, they resembled *Homo erectus* more than us. We traded this ridge for a wider forehead, and maybe this was the feature that made *Homo sapiens* look wise.

Since the early 2010s, more evidence and theories have piled up about what happened to this extinct species. The Neanderthals are a hot and contested topic in contemporary prehistoric research. Whereas it was once thought that Neanderthals sustained themselves exclusively by hunting large animals, now it is clear that their diet was much more diverse. They ate plants and roots, fished all kinds of fish, and even dined out on a smorgasbord of seafood. The discovery of seashells at Neanderthal habitation sites suggests that they were capable swimmers and divers. Although they could have made do with shells that washed up on the beach, the Neanderthals insisted on fresher food from deep underwater.

Even though Neanderthals, like us, ate whatever they could find, their massive physique and living conditions during successive ice ages required them to consume many more calories. How many more? About 1,000 more a day. It is hard to squeeze so much energy out of roots and plants, and Neanderthal life undoubtedly depended on large mammals, especially mammoths. When mammoths disappeared, Neanderthals were in clear and immediate danger.

But until then, the Neanderthals enjoyed rich and fulfilling lives and left behind evidence of their complicated interrelationship with the world, which went far beyond matters of diet and survival. They engaged in nimble finger-work and created jewelry and body ornaments out of bones and the claws of birds of prey. A hundred and sixty thousand years ago they entered the bowels of a dark cave (Bruniquel Cave in France) and built a mysterious ring out of stalagmites and stalactites; they left footprints in the volcanic ash at the top of a volcano that erupted in Italy 350,000 years ago, as a message for future generations that they were there. And they took care of their sick and needy. The discovery of the bones of Neanderthals with disabilities and birth defects who lived to a relatively old age shows that members of Neanderthal groups must have supported them for many years—a kind of Paleolithic national insurance. They were characters and it would be interesting to go back in time and visit them.

The most tantalizing and perhaps most significant new piece of information is that we are all, dear readers, a little bit Neanderthal ourselves. The genome of modern-day human beings living outside of Africa contains 2–4 per cent of material from this extinct species. This means that the two kinds of humans—chinned and chinless, *Homo sapiens* and Neanderthal—intermixed. This means that they also . . . well, OK, you get the point. And one of the places where they probably had such liaisons was right there, on the western slopes of Mount Carmel in the caves of Wadi el-Mughara.

***

During the long excavations that she oversaw, Dorothy Garrod identified seven distinct archeological layers in the El-Wad Cave: seven layers of continuous human existence, from the Neanderthals who were there around 50,000 years ago to the last hunter-gatherers who roamed there some 15,000 years ago. In the Tabun Cave, the continuous human settlement was even more impressive: a 23m-deep (76ft) stratigraphic column (sequence of archeological layers), one of the deepest ever discovered in prehistoric caves.

The stone tool technology unearthed in the Tabun Cave excavations was wedged between the Levallois spearheads from 50,000 years ago in the upper strata and the earliest hand axes in the lower levels. It was akin to finding a modern building where the constantly changing residents had left an iPhone 4 on the living room table and Alexander Graham Bell's telephone in the basement. And this is hardly the best analogy considering that only 150 years separated Bell's device and the iPhone, whereas the stone tools at the top and bottom "floors" were made hundreds of thousands of years apart. Hundreds of thousands of years in which humans went to sleep and woke up in the same cave.

In the upper layers of the Tabun Cave, Garrod made a sensational discovery alongside the Levallois spearheads: the remains of both a Neanderthal woman and a *Homo sapiens* man, comprising her nearly complete skull and his jawbone. Surprisingly, the Neanderthal skull was found in a layer *above* the one with the modern jawbone, which means that Neanderthals lived in the cave after *Homo sapiens*, not before them. This revelation painted a completely different picture from the accepted one in Europe, and it changed the face of prehistory. Later findings at other sites bolstered and corroborated Garrod's conclusions.

And that's not all. Garrod discovered that in the Tabun Cave, Neanderthals and *Homo sapiens* shared culture and behavior. They led almost identical lives and made the same flint tools. *Homo sapiens* made tools with the Levallois technique, which their neighbors in the cave apparently also used. The discovery of this partnership was almost totally different from everything assumed beforehand.

In the excavation season of 1929, Kitson Clark, the researcher who had just recovered from ehrlichiosis, was sent to check the Es-Skhul Cave at the top of the wadi—a cave that barely appeared in the delegation's initial work plan. There too, they found Levallois spearheads next to additional evidence of intensive human activity. Three years later, excavations at the same site unearthed the remains of ten humans (adults and children), believed to be the earliest *Homo sapiens* ever discovered outside of Africa. But they were not completely identical to modern humans. All the skeletons had anatomical features that seemed to belong to an earlier species. It is highly likely that they belonged to a mixed *Homo sapiens*–Neanderthal population who lived on Mount Carmel 100,000 years ago and then passed down their genes, including to us.

Homo sapiens and Neanderthals diverged, it seems, from a common ancestor. It used to be popularly believed that this shared ancestor lived in Africa and Europe some 400,000–500,000 years ago. Like almost everything in archeology, this belief has long been cast into doubt. And not just doubt, but the kind that raises the stakes. A study based on dental evolution that examined over 900 prehistoric teeth from dozens of different individuals—modern and archaic humans alike—showed that according to the rate of change, the split happened as early as 800,000 years ago. This model opened a wide door to new interpretations of the differences between the two species, because they had several more hundred years in which to diverge and grow in different directions. On the other hand, if indeed nearly a million years of evolution separated these two human species, how is it possible that 50,000 years ago, they were still capable of interbreeding? An abundance of genetic and behavioral limitations should have developed to prevent such a possibility.

If this were not complicated enough, in 2008 another human species was discovered in the Altai Mountains in Siberia: the Denisovans. The Neanderthals had similar relations with them as well. When a Denisovan girl's fingerbones were examined, it was discovered that while her mother was a Denisovan, her father was a Neanderthal. These characters seem to have had a much better reputation than the one we have lumbered them with over the past 200 years.

***

The most intriguing question about the Neanderthals is why they disappeared. After all, they were strong, robust, organized, and at least as smart as us. Nevertheless, we are still here and they went extinct. This did not happen because of us: we did not eat them, nor did we throw them in the sea. There is no evidence or finding that supports such a story, and as we have seen, it seems that we got along with them quite well. So, what happened to them?

One of the most interesting theories pins the blame on their small population size and enormous geographic dispersion. It is estimated that when *Homo sapiens* appeared in their midst, the Neanderthal population was no larger than a few tens of thousands (and some argue, even smaller), and these were subdivided into groups that had no contact with each other. One group lived in the valleys of the Alps, a second near the Rhine, and a third in modern-day Kazakhstan. Genetic studies of Neanderthal bones support the theory that these were distinct regional populations and suggest that each had at most

3,000–4,000 members at any given time. Computer simulations of population groups with similar numbers cast serious doubt on their survival prospects.

In the Sidrón Cave in the limestone hills of the Asturias region of Spain, archeologists have discovered the remains of a group of Neanderthals who were apparently killed by another group. The large victim count made it possible to run parallel genetic testing. What emerged was that some of them had been born as a result of inbreeding. Prehistoric incest. Many of them suffered from all sorts of deformities and disabilities. This seems to have been a common phenomenon among Neanderthals, not least because of their relative isolation, and it certainly did no favors for their demographic wellbeing.

Researchers believe that the Allee effect also contributed to the Neanderthals' plight. This is a common phenomenon in small groups: they are forced to invest a great deal of time and energy risking their lives in activities like hunting and protecting themselves from predators. The number of individuals who reach sexual maturity is therefore low compared to other, larger groups. Moreover, the smaller the group, the weaker its resistance to random disasters. Drought, serious diseases, and climate change are misfortunes from which large groups can recover. But they can eradicate smaller animal groups, including human populations.

Besides all this and the disappearance of the mammoths—problems that they might have overcome somehow—the Neanderthals also had some bad luck. That bad luck was us, *Homo sapiens*. Our intrusion into their habitats 50,000 years ago certainly did not help them. We widened the geographic pockets between different Neanderthal groups and competed with them for the same resources and lands. Wadi el-Mughara, it seems, got a bit crowded.

Homo sapiens were thinner, lighter, more numerous, and better suited to hunting small and fast animals. Our intentions were not necessarily bad, but from the Neanderthals' perspective the outcome was.

***

The Port of Haifa was inaugurated on October 31, 1933. The event was supposed to be full of pomp and circumstance, but bloody riots between Jews and Arabs had erupted in the city a few days earlier and the party was called off.

Dorothy Garrod's excavations at Wadi el-Mughara and her classic book *The Stone Age of Mount Carmel* paved her way to the Disney Professorship of Archeology at the University of Cambridge (no relation to the animation giant). This had been a men's-only job, and Garrod's appointment in 1939 was nothing less than an academic earthquake and a gender revolution.

As far as we know today, the last Neanderthals were concentrated in the region of Gibraltar at the tip of the Iberian Peninsula. In Gorhan's Cave, a world heritage site on the limestone cliffs that kiss the sea in front of the Straits of Gibraltar within sight of Africa, evidence has been found of a Neanderthal presence until 28,000 years ago, which is closer to our time than anywhere else on earth. They ate fish, hunted mammals, and trapped many kinds of birds—some for their feathers, which were used in various rituals. Perhaps these early humans chose this site because they could see the continent their distant ancestors had departed from; perhaps they were pushed there by other groups; or perhaps it was simply a wonderful place to live. It was quite the retirement home.

Ever since these Neanderthals disappeared, we have been alone. But we are convinced that the world not only belongs to us but was created to satisfy our needs. We have done, and continue to do, amazing things on this planet. We have climbed mountains, sent manned submarines down into the depths of the ocean, reached the moon, split the atom, and produced thirty seasons of *The Simpsons* to watch on demand. But we are also laying waste to the planet we live on. We do what we fancy, as if there were no tomorrow and nobody on earth but us.

And that's true: there *is* nobody else. If there were still Neanderthals, Denisovans, or anyone else, perhaps we would behave slightly differently. We would have had someone else to look at, like the classroom bully who realizes he doesn't have to mess things up for the other kids just because he can. Maybe we could have learned something from another human species living alongside us, instead of marching with unwavering confidence from what was once paradise toward a chilling future.

Dorothy Garrod (center) and Francis Turville-Petre (right) during the excavations at the Carmel Caves, 1931

CHAPTER 6

UNDERWORLD

50,000–30,000 years ago

From Manot Cave in Israel's western Galilee to France's Dordogne Valley

Where and when did *Homo sapiens* emerge? What can we learn from cave art? Why is touching rock such a powerful experience? And how does the Western Wall fit into all of this?

The entrance is slightly elliptical, like the door to a fairy's house or a monster's lair in a children's storybook. But it didn't have to take this shape. There are many different types of cave openings: some are barely visible, mere cracks in the rock that you have to wriggle through, while others are wide and inviting. Some look like windows or skylights; others cannot be seen at all and only by accident or chance reveal themselves to the world. Many of these openings must be climbed into; others are entered by descending with ropes and harnesses; and there are some—among the most beautiful and intriguing in the world—that one must dive into. The entrance is a liminal zone. Behind it lies another world.

You notice the difference as soon as you step in. The temperature changes. It's chilly, moist. Even if the sun is beating down outside and the earth is dry, inside it is pleasant. As you take one cautious step, then another, venturing into totally foreign terrain, your eyes struggle to adjust to the darkness, which will only intensify. Without a headlamp—or long ago before our time, without flaming torches—it would be scary to stray from the entrance.

Your headlamp reveals a huge cavern of several dozen square meters, with rocky, downward-sloping walls. Like the opening, this too comes in more than one shape and size. Sometimes it is a long and narrow tunnel, with lots of twists and turns; or there may be several caverns at different levels, and you can't always walk upright, certainly not the whole way down. At some point, you will need to stop, get on all fours, and even crawl on your belly. To move down, up, sideways. Here, if you pause for a moment at the bottom of your descent from the big grotto, you can hear the sound of water trickling, a constant drip-drip, the hypnotizing soundtrack of karst: the sedimentary rock that sculpts the majestic vistas of the Pyrenees in southwestern Europe, the Julian Alps in Slovenia, the Yorkshire moors in Britain, the Wulong region of China, the Yucatán Peninsula in Mexico, the Appalachians in the Americas, and in Israel, the entire area from the southern Judean Desert up to the heights of the Upper Galilee. The permeable, cavernous limestone promises treasures and discoveries. Only when you switch off your headlamp, when the darkness takes over not just your sight but also your mind—only then can you say you're there.

Welcome to the Underworld. It's a hidden, unfamiliar, threatening, enticing, enormous world, both dark and beautiful. More specifically: welcome to Manot Cave, a few miles south of the international border between Israel and Lebanon. Home, 50,000 or maybe 60,000 years ago, to people just like us.

***

Manot Cave is breathtakingly beautiful and rich with stalagmites and stalactites. It was discovered by chance in 2008 (such discoveries are almost always made by accident, and that accident almost always involves a tractor or a bulldozer). It gained worldwide fame, at least among prehistorians, thanks to a *Homo sapiens* skull dated to a significant period in human history: 55,000 years before our time. This was a time when there were apparently still Neanderthals there, just before modern humans reached Europe from Africa via the Levantine corridor. In this respect, it is as if this skull were placed in the inner sanctum of Manot Cave to fit the conventional timeline of the history of *Homo sapiens*. Of all the theories about thorny and controversial prehistoric questions, some of which we have already presented here (Why did we climb down from trees? Hunting versus scavenging; the hand axe enigma; who were the Neanderthals? And when did humans begin to master fire?), one theory that remains relatively stable and agreed upon concerns the emergence of *Homo sapiens* and their exodus from Africa.

"Human history at last took off around 50,000 years ago, at the time of what I have termed our Great Leap Forward," writes Jared Diamond in his book *Guns, Germs, and Steel*. Diamond notes that the evidence of this "Great Leap Forward" comes from sites in East Africa where archeologists have discovered a few stone tools and ostrich eggshells, which would soon make an appearance in the Levant and then in western Europe. Yuval Noah Harari, the man who propelled *Homo sapiens* to the top of international bestseller lists, clarifies in a much more up-to-date book than Diamond's that "most scientists agree that by 150,000 years ago, East Africa was populated by Sapiens that looked just like us . . . Scientists also agree that about 70,000 years ago, Sapiens from East Africa spread into the Arabian peninsula, and from there they quickly overran the entire Eurasian landmass."

So, humanity's "birthplace" remained fixed, and only the timing of its exodus got pushed back by a few tens of thousands of years. All the rest remained a mystery, or as Bill Bryson puts it: "These first modern humans are surprisingly shadowy. We know less about ourselves, curiously enough, than about almost any other line of hominids." Bryson is right. Not only do we know less about ourselves, but we are also asking less. It's as if human researchers, *Homo sapiens* in the flesh, were only waiting for evidence of their direct ancestors and immediately and warmly embraced them and placed them at the top of the human dynasty without asking too many questions. "Good thing you made it, guys, you wouldn't *believe* the folks we had to deal with before."

In 1868, five skeletons were discovered in the Dordogne Valley in France, in a rock shelter known as Cro-Magnon. This happened some ten years after human remains were discovered in the Neander Valley in Germany and were therefore named "Neanderthals." There was no avoiding a comparison between the remains unearthed in both valleys. Those from the Dordogne were strikingly taller and more refined than the Neanderthals: they had round skulls and prominent chins, and they were missing the brow ridge that was so typical of the other species. Most importantly: they looked a lot like modern Europeans. You could have taken a glance at these ancient skeletons and said, "Hey, that looks like someone I used to know."

Next to the Cro-Magnons, as this species was named (nowadays, they would have been classified as *Homo sapiens*), archeologists found flint tools that were totally different from those used by Neanderthals. The most common and advanced tool was a knife, or a "blade" in the scientific jargon, an instrument almost as elegant as the people who forged it, which is why it is considered a wonder of prehistoric enterprise. The fact that the Neanderthals never crafted such blades made it easy to dismiss them as an inferior species.

But it was the Cro-Magnons' cave drawings that positioned them at the top of the evolutionary pedestal. The first ones discovered were in the Cave of Altamira in northern Spain in 1879. In time, countless subterranean chambers were discovered in other parts of Spain and southern France, and on their rock walls was an impressive array of images of animals. These were and still are spectacular and exciting discoveries and these caves have earned their status as must-see attractions for so many tourists from all over the world.

"After Altamira, all is decadence," said Pablo Picasso when he visited there.

Owing to the flint knives discovered in these caves, there was no doubt that the world's first artists were not Neanderthals but Cro-Magnons. It was they who painted with such impressive precision; it was they who engraved images in color on these walls, which we can all connect to, see what they contain, and wholeheartedly call works of art, just like those displayed in the galleries and museums that we ourselves have built. From there, it was only a short hop to giving them, and us, the name "*Homo sapiens*": "wise human."

But this name, however appropriate, did not answer the most pressing and fundamental questions: when did *Homo sapiens* begin to develop? How did this happen? And most importantly, *why* did this happen? Why did a new species of humans emerge? Everyone knew that we came from Africa, but not much more than this. The first significant discoveries with the potential to answer these questions were made only in the early twenty-first century.

In 2003, Tim White, one of the world's preeminent fossil experts, went digging in the Awash Valley in Ethiopia and discovered three modern-looking human skulls, dated to 160,000 years ago. White proposed that these were the direct ancestors of *Homo sapiens* in East Africa. He called them *Homo sapiens idaltu*, using the word for "elder" in the language of Ethiopia's Afar people. Curiously, next to these skulls, he also discovered flint tools associated with an earlier period, as well as technologies that seemed much more advanced, associated with the next human generation. It was like discovering the skeleton of a medieval human next to a papyrus scroll and a typewriter, or next to a spear and a handgun. Past, present, and future, all rolled into one.

Only two years after White's arresting discovery was published in the prestigious journal *Nature*, the no-less-prestigious journal *Science* responded with a breakthrough discovery of its own: even more ancient remains of *Homo sapiens* had been found on the banks of the Omo River in western Ethiopia. In truth, the findings themselves—skull fragments—had been known back in the mid-1960s, but incorrectly dated. The thought of going back to re-examine these skull fragments with cutting-edge methods might have been motivated by the rivalry between the two journals, but the results were unequivocal: these humans lived 195,000 years before our time! No less importantly, this was 30,000 years before their northeastern neighbors, *Homo sapiens idaltu*. From this point on, modern scholars converged on the consensus that *Homo sapiens* first appeared in Africa some 200,000 years ago.

This evidence matched the findings of ground-breaking studies into ancient DNA, which used data from the placentas of women all over the world. The genetic sequencing showed that Mitochondrial Eve—the mother of all modern humans—lived in Africa around the same time as the hypothesized appearance of *Homo sapiens*. This also solved misunderstandings about two caves in Israel: Es-Skhul and Qafzeh, where archeologists found the remains of *Homo sapiens*-like humans, who lived some 100,000 years ago. Suddenly everything fell into place perfectly. *Homo sapiens* began their journey in East Africa some 200,000 years ago, left Africa in several waves of migration—to caves in the Carmel and Galilee regions—and continued marching on to Europe, where they were patiently awaited by the Neanderthals.

One problem remained, which was not so straightforward: the vast cultural differences between the abilities of *Homo sapiens* living in Africa and the Levant and those of their descendants who reached modern-day France and Spain. More specifically, where did the cave drawings of those once known as the Cro-Magnons come from? To understand the power and importance of these drawings, we had to pack our suitcases and venture further afield.

***

We really needed to stop for coffee at the airport exit in Bordeaux. There were a few decent options, but as always when more than two people are on a trip, the easiest thing is to put off decisions and plow on because there might be something better on the way. It was early on a Sunday morning, and the dream of having a cup of coffee with a freshly baked pastry evaporated the further our rented car took us toward our destination: the Dordogne Valley.

When the great American novelist Henry Miller took a break from his routine and went on a long tour of the Greek islands, he made a point of stopping on the way in this breathtaking region of France. "I had long wanted to visit the valley of the Dordogne," he explained in *The Colossus of Maroussi*. "Just to glimpse the black, mysterious river at Dômme from the beautiful bluff at the edge of the town is something to be grateful for all one's life . . . It is the country of enchantment which the poets have staked out and which they alone may lay claim to. It is the nearest thing to Paradise . . . Actually, it must have been a paradise for many thousands of years. I believe it must have been so for the Cro-Magnon man."

The primordial charm of this valley in the traditionalist heart of France has not faded in the seventy or eighty years since Miller's formative visit. The Dordogne, which contains the densest cluster of cave paintings in the world, gives visitors the impression that its landscape has looked exactly the same since time immemorial, more or less, with the same rounded peaks, the same natural rock shelters, the same winding rivers through thick and heavy soil. It's an absolute paradise. But still, a cup of coffee would have been a great addition. Even a single espresso. *We'll get a drink when we get to the cave,* say those for whom a caffeine deficit does not make their temples contract into their brains, and who can enjoy the view while munching on a pear they remembered to pack from home. *There must be a cafeteria or a canteen at the entrance,* they chirp.

When we reached the entrance at the end of a narrow road snaking down from the village, there was nobody there and certainly no café. It was not tourist season, and most tourists are dropped off anyway by air-conditioned buses to stand in line for the famous Lascaux Cave. Or rather not for the cave itself, which is closed to visitors, but for a perfect replica built right next door. It's a bit like a prehistoric Disneyland, only instead of an attraction that looks like something imaginary, this is something imaginary that looks like something real. We'll get there later, but now a young man on a bicycle rides toward us. He will sell us our tickets, switch on the lights, and guide us through the cave that we have come all the way here to see: Rouffignac Cave.

The existence of this cave and the possibility that it might contain prehistoric paintings were mentioned in various writings as early as the sixteenth century. Hikers and tourists visited some of its caverns in the nineteenth and early twentieth centuries. But only in 1956 did Louis-René Nougier and Romain Robert, two prehistorians from the French Pyrenees, enter the caves and identify and verify the diverse drawings of animals on the walls. The cave was opened to the public in 1959 and quickly became known as the Cave of the Hundred Mammoths (although there are many more mammoths on the walls—over 150, in fact). When it comes to visual representations of this magnificent, tusked beast, Rouffignac Cave is utterly peerless.

The cave stood untouched for millennia. It was preserved and is now presented to the public unchanged, except for one minor detail: a train runs straight through it. On the tracks are little carriages with seats that swivel depending on the direction of travel and the nearest attractions. "Voilà, here on the right are two mammoths and a bison!" says the guide, and the chairs rotate to face the drawings, so that nobody misses them as the carriages glide forward into the next section of the cave. Thankfully for us, the train operator (and tour guide and ticket salesman, all rolled in one) is sensitive to our frustration, perhaps because we are practically the only people there. He agrees to break protocol and lets us jump out of the carriages for a few minutes.

The train stops at a depth of several hundred meters, far from the cave's opening. It is pitch black, and the darkness envelops us like a thick blanket. Within a few seconds, we lose any sense of orientation or direction—there is no left or right or any idea where the cave continues. All we know is that our feet are on the ground. Everyone chuckles anxiously. *Come on, monsieur, please light a torch so we can see where we are . . .*

These railway tracks were installed because tourists would not walk hundreds of meters underground, not even to see a thousand mammoths. But this journey *was* made by prehistoric humans, and they had good reasons for venturing as deep down as this. They insisted on expressing themselves in a place where it is doubtful anyone else could have seen their work. They could have painted much more comfortably close to the cave's opening, with natural lighting and ventilation, but they don't seem to have been interested in any of this. Neither in the comfort, nor in the natural lighting.

When our guide switches on the lights, we see that prehistoric humans not only climbed down to these depths but squeezed into the narrowest parts of the cave, and it was only there—where there is no room to stand or even to kneel, but only to crawl on one's belly—that they produced the most beautiful paintings of mammoths in the cave.

The French prehistorian Jean Clottes, the doyen of the study of cave art, argues that for early humans, "going into deep caves to paint or engrave their walls . . . was deliberately venturing into a supernatural world for practical purposes." Clottes, who has written over twenty books about cave art and published hundreds of scientific papers, explains that torches or grease lamps "would constantly cast shadows on walls that were never straight, but full of mysterious hollows and reliefs that briefly came to life." In the subterranean tunnels of Rouffignac, it is easy to imagine what Clottes was describing even when holding an LED light instead of a burning grease lamp.

When we met him a year or two before visiting Rouffignac, Clottes launched, for the umpteenth time, into stories about his countless experiences in the caves he had explored: from the Cave of Niaux at the foot of the Pyrenees, which he reached in 1974, to the most celebrated and electrifying of his discoveries, Chauvet Cave. It was New Year's Eve in 1994, and Clottes, who was France's General Inspector of Archeology at the time, was about to go on a long-awaited family vacation. The suitcases were already in the car when a cave hobbyist by the name of Jean-Marie Chauvet called to tell him to drop everything and come to see something immediately.

Chauvet belonged to a rare breed of people who get a kick out of burrowing underground. The open-air—mountains, valleys, glistening lakes, cows grazing on verdant meadows—does nothing for them. They spend days on end in areas rich in karst, searching for cracks through which they can slip into dark and unknown caverns. Some walk carrying a goose feather in their hands or stuck to their backpacks, trying to use it to detect barely perceptible gusts from the belly of the earth. That week, Chauvet and two of his friends had explored the rocky landscape around Vallon-Pont-d'Arc in the Ardèche region. They spotted an unfamiliar fissure with air escaping through it, and they decided to try to wriggle in. After eight hours of clearing chunks of rock, lumps of earth, and piles of boulders, they had an opening wide enough for them to squeeze through. At first, they saw nothing special, only a big empty space with stalagmites and stalactites, which they had already seen more than enough of. They walked a few meters deeper into the cave, descended a level, and held their breath. What they saw was enough to convince them not to take another step before getting Jean Clottes on the scene.

Clottes drove for 400km (249mi), not exactly thrilled and having few expectations. He had seen enough impressive caves in his life—and he had been summoned enough times to see potential sites where the only mammoths were mammoth disappointments. Moreover, his vacation had promised a much more exciting way to celebrate New Year's Eve than driving along winding roads from his home in the Pyrenees to the

A stone tool from Ubeidiya (ch. 1)

Early humans dated to almost 2 million yeras ago discovered at Dmanisi site (under the roof) (ch. 1)

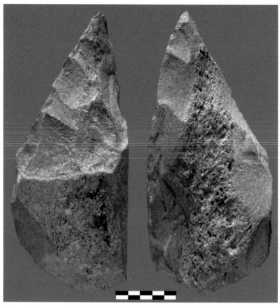

An elephant bone modified as a hand axe at Castel di Guido, Italy (ch. 2)

An unexplained plentiful of magnificent handaxes at Boxgrove, UK (ch. 2)

Excavations at Lower Paleolithic Daughters of Jacob Bridge (ch. 2)

Handaxe, prehistoric enigma and shining polyaster at Pompidou center, Paris

A quarry and stone-tool workshop at the Paleolithic home depot at Mt.Pua, Israel (ch. 3)

Innovative stone tools technologies manifested in flint blades at Qesem Cave, Israel (ch. 4)

Qesem Cave, protected under the shade, alongside road no. 5, Israel (ch. 4)

One of the last Neanderthal refugia at Vanguard Cave, Gibraltar (ch. 5)

Animals depicted at one of the most marveleous panels at Chauvet Cave (ch. 6)

The home of homo sapiens some 50,000 years ago. Excavations at Manot cave (ch. 6)

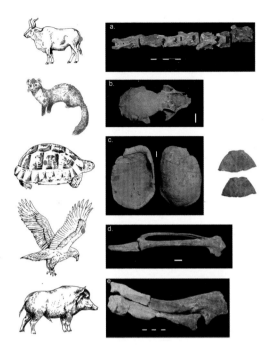

Animal remains unearthed at the Shaman burial of Hilazon Cave, Israel (ch. 7)

Dandan Bolotin in the midst of a shamanic ritual, Ecuador (ch. 7)

The Nahal Mishmar Hoard of the Chalcolithic period (ch. 9)

The trench in Jericho, excavated by Kenyon, with the tower overlooking the mountain peak (ch. 8)

Timna copper mines, Israel (ch. 9)

The passge leading to the inner chamber at Rujum el hiri, Israel (ch. 10)

Ardèche. When he reached the rendezvous point with Chauvet and his friends, they told him he would need to enter the cave without a helmet or a coat. The passages were too narrow, and every centimeter counted. Clottes forced his way in, following the original discoverers, and in the first subterranean chamber he saw a drawing of a big, black panther and a hyena—two wild animals not depicted in any other cave. Deeper in, he encountered an ancient rhinoceros drawn with such vivid precision that the way it was adapted to the rock relief made it look almost three-dimensional. In the next section of the cave, he saw a breathtaking panel of horse heads tightly packed together. "I had tears in my eyes," Clottes recalls, as if he had been there just a moment before.

The same day, Clottes insisted on calling the French culture minister. He informed him of the discovery of a stunning cave, with artworks just as rich as those in the Lascaux Cave, which is rightfully known as the "Sistine Chapel of the prehistoric world." Like Lascaux, Chauvet Cave—named for the man who smuggled himself in—is closed to visitors. France learned a lesson from the more than 100,000 tourists who shuffled through Lascaux's caverns over the years, causing considerable damage. The German movie director Werner Herzog was invited to record the last public visit at Chauvet, for a film called *Cave of Forgotten Dreams*, and ever since, one can only join the masses of tourists waiting for their turn to visit a replica of the original cave. In terms of its appearance and the structure of the caverns, the replica is indeed accurate. But in terms of the feeling—the emotional experience—it would be better to be buffeted around in a theme park ride, as in Rouffignac Cave. Because in the replica, perfect as it may be, the walls are made of plaster, the stalagmites and stalactites are 3-D printouts made using computer imaging, and the paintings are copies by contemporary artists.

After six years of documenting and studying Chauvet Cave, Clottes proved that what made it unique was not just the panther, the hyena, and the rhinoceros depictions on the walls.

These images were dated to a much earlier period than any other caves containing such art: 37,000–33,500 years ago for the first burst of creativity at the site, and another round some 31,000–28,000 years ago. That would make it twice as old as Lascaux, which is dated to 17,000 years ago, and much more ancient than Rouffignac, whose painted mammoths are a mere 13,000 years old.

In this respect, Chauvet Cave pulled the rug out from under much of modern research. It proved that humanity's artistic abilities—and more importantly its need to pursue visual expression deep underground—were facts of *Homo sapiens*'s life around the time of its estimated arrival in western Europe. In terms of the conventional migration flowcharts, it is quite possible our distant ancestors who decorated Chauvet Cave had nurtured or even just started to develop these talents and needs during their sojourn in the Levant, in caves such as Manot; and that their descendants, who according to the same flowcharts probably made the reverse journey back to the Levant, could have brought such elements with them back from Europe. The fact that prehistoric drawings have not been found at Manot or in any other cave in the Levant does not necessarily mean that their inhabitants lacked these needs and abilities or lost them on the way. Maybe we just need to look harder to find them.

***

The most interesting question about these cave drawings is, of course, what they all meant. This question has exercised generations of scholars, ever since the first drawings were discovered on the walls of Altamira. The first explanation was, unsurprisingly, that these were forgeries—there was no way that early humans could have been so talented. There were even people who testified under oath that local painters had been commissioned to produce this art, for suitable payment. When more cave drawings were discovered around Altamira and in more distant regions, the skeptics were forced to admit their mistake and make way for theories offered by serious and responsible scholarship.

The first widely accepted theory was that this was art for art's sake: that these images were drawn solely out of the artists' urge for self-expression. Just as modern-day artists set up their easels and express themselves through brushstrokes, humans did something similar thousands of years ago. According to a more popular theory, the cave drawings were part of a ritual that gave people a sense of power and mastery over the animal world before hunting expeditions. There is also a territorial explanation: the depictions had an informational purpose. They were symbols of ownership or ancient tribal identity. Something like American license plates, with symbols of the states where the vehicles are registered, or road signs at the entrances to towns, which proudly announce the number of inhabitants and recommended local attractions.

After all these tantalizing explanations and theories, we should return to the bowels of Rouffignac Cave and Jean Clottes's insights.

The drawings at Rouffignac are, as mentioned before, a long way from the entrance. The total darkness, alcoves, and claw marks on the walls show that this was once the abode of ferocious cave bears. It would have taken courage and determination to make it this far. The walls of the cave twist and turn at unexpected angles, and the flickering torchlight must have created a mesmerizing effect, bringing the inanimate to life, rousing the spirits. Jean Clottes and David Lewis-Williams, the South African anthropologist who was Clottes's mentor and partner in researching and deciphering cave drawings, propose that the act of entering the caves and drawing animals on their walls was a spiritual practice. Something akin to what the West considers religion or religious faith. The dominance of megafauna in these pictures reflected their importance in the world these humans inhabited: just like the importance of the hand axes crafted from elephant bones in the lives of *Homo erectus*. These humans undoubtedly told countless stories about their deeds, about the origins of panthers and mammoths, and about their ferocious power.

"Faith in the supranatural power contained in the walls of these caves was literally vital to the creation of so many pictures," explains Clottes, clarifying that early humans believed that the animals' spirits resided in the walls themselves. By painting or engraving the rock, early humans not only interacted with these wild beasts but genuinely grasped their power. The rock was a screen, inside which and beyond which lay a creature of immense power. It is no coincidence that so many handprints have been found on cave walls, and so many bones were found shoved into cracks in the rock. Touch was essential.

This concept is certainly reminiscent of something familiar to the whole Jewish world, and the charming scholar of cave paintings cannot resist making a comparison to the Western Wall in Jerusalem. There too, physically touching a stone wall is an important ritual, and there too messages are shoved into crevices in an ancient wall full of such splendor and spirituality.

It is possible, therefore, that what prehistoric humans painted on the cave walls was not depictions of what they found in abundance around them, but images of what was missing— the animals that they prayed would return. In the region of Périgord, where Rouffignac Cave is located, almost one-third of images of animals on cave walls are mammoths, but when they were drawn or engraved 13,000 years ago, mammoths were already teetering on the brink of extinction. They were presumably much more alive in the collective memory of their artists than in the open spaces above the caves.

By physically touching the cave walls, beyond which they believed that these animals existed, early humans hoped to tease them out from within and make them return to their world. The flickering torchlight, accurate drawings adapted to the texture of the relief, and the narrow oxygen-poor caverns— all this excited the senses and would have made the pictures of mammoths and rhinoceroses come to life. Lewis-Williams attributes the practice of cave drawings to ancient trance rituals.

A doctoral student in archeology who joined our tour of the Dordogne seeks to prove in her research that early humans entered altered states of consciousness when they descended into these caves. They went into the caves fully conscious but soon slipped into a state of hypoxia as their torches consumed the thin oxygen. This might sound like a speculative avenue of inquiry, but underpinning it is an understanding of the importance attached to broadening human consciousness in every culture and at every time.

Scientists recently published some surprising discoveries from Pinwheel Cave in California, where Native Americans lived some 400 years ago. In crevices, they found dozens of quids (chewing resin), munched by the cave-dwellers and stuck to the ceiling. Laboratory tests have proven beyond doubt that the quids were chewed pieces of datura, a plant with powerful hallucinogenic properties. Besides chewing gum, the cave's ancient inhabitants also left behind a bright red painting of a datura flower on the ceiling—unequivocal archeological evidence of the ancient connection between matter and spirit.

It is easy to fantasize in the bowels of a narrow cave, even if you have entered on a train ride with a pocket light in hand. Maybe not about mammoths and bison, but definitely about something like a hot cup of coffee. Thankfully the multi-tasking guide showing us around the caverns of Rouffignac also pointed us to an excellent restaurant at the top of the road offering suitable culinary compensation, including an espresso and a pear tart for dessert. From there, we continued to other caves, with names such as Font-de-Gaume, Pech Merle, Les Combarelles, Cognac, and for those who still had the strength, also replicas of Chauvet and Lascaux. It was a wonderful week both in the heavenly landscapes above and in the thought-provoking, mind-bending caverns below. But the answer to the question that led us to the Dordogne, about the vastly different capacities for religious expression among the inhabitants of western Europe and of the Levant, was waiting for us elsewhere. In Africa, of course.

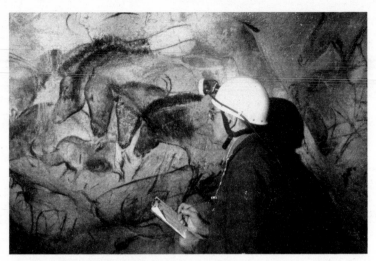

Jean Clottes in front of one of the panels at Chauvet Cave, France

CHAPTER 7

MEMENTO MORI

12,000 years ago

**From the Hilazon Cave in the Lower Galilee to the
Ecuadorian jungle**

**When did humans start burying their dead? Who was
the woman for whose sake ninety tortoises were sacrificed?
And who is worth taking along on an ayahuasca trip?**

Someone has died. Someone beloved, certainly by his close
family—his parents, children, and siblings. Someone who did
a lot in life: mostly good things, even important ones. The
funeral procession moves slowly from the dead man's house or
the funeral parlor toward his final resting place. At the cemetery,
someone recites a familiar prayer. Here and there, people crying
and choking up, and the occasional howl of pain pierces the
silence. The deceased is lowered in a coffin or a shroud into
a grave. Everything is restrained and respectful, with neat
pathways and lawns, as if the dead cared about nothing more
than scrupulously pruned hedges.

Some 12,000 years ago, such a scene would have looked totally
different. Leore Grosman, an archeologist from the Hebrew
University of Jerusalem, leads us to a site she has unearthed and
explored in the Hilazon Cave and describes a wild and ecstatic
funeral that took place there. The funeral of a short woman with
deformities from birth and unique social status.

"There was a big group here," explains Grosman, "200–300
people, coming up here with all sorts of objects in tow. If we
could have watched them, we'd probably have seen that each

person was carrying something, and all in all, together, they hauled up quite a cargo. In my opinion, they'd been preparing for this journey for a long time."

—*What did they bring with them?*

"Day-to-day tools. Tools that became sanctified by being brought on the journey. They didn't bring anything that wasn't already familiar to them. That's quite clear. They brought lots of geodes, for example, which are a kind of really pretty, amorphous stone with quartz inside, and there's some just around the corner. They brought household utensils and mostly lots of animals."

—*What animals?*

"Ninety tortoises, for example."

—*Ninety?!*

"At least. And two martens and three cows. They all got here alive."

—*Including the tortoises?*

"Yes. They had to be collected one by one over quite a long time and brought to the cave, and there was definitely an enclosure here where they were kept, so they wouldn't be scuttling around everyone's feet."

—*And that's just the animals that arrived whole, right?*

"Right. Besides these animals, they also brought gazelles, it's not clear how many, but lots. Also, an eagle wing, half a leopard pelvis, and maybe also a snake."

—*Why "maybe"?*

"Because it might have made its own way in, after everyone else. Personally, I'm sure they brought it as well, but that's hard to prove."

—*And what did they do with them, with all this wildlife?*

"They ate them. Cooked them, roasted them, and ate them."

—*Including the tortoises?*

"Of course! They cut them all the same way, by slicing their bellies and disconnecting their innards from the shell. Only after they had finished eating them did they bury their shells and the other objects in the grave."

—Sounds like that took a long time.

"It was a long, drawn-out event. In my opinion, they designed this place in advance, to suit their needs. They dug pits in the cave and arranged rocky platforms around them. The cave entrance looked like an amphitheater."

The ascent to the Hilazon Cave is not easy. The snaking, uphill path is exhausting. The cave entrance cannot be seen from the dry river valley and only reveals itself in the last few feet of the way up. It's surprising and certainly impressive even when you step out of a rented car, carrying just a bottle of water and a healthy pumpernickel sandwich. The people who climbed up here thousands of years ago dragged along equipment weighing dozens of kilos, bringing a few dozen live tortoises and at least three wild cows, which must have trampled on the hard soil with their hooves, whipping up clouds of dust and amplifying the commotion. They came not only to bury their dead but also for a meaningful spiritual event, marked with a long grilled-meat banquet.

Grosman first visited the Hilazon Cave as a master's degree student, when she was asked to check if there was anything interesting in the cave on the slopes of the valley. It was in the mid-1990s, and the cave was used by local Bedouins as a shelter for their herds of goats and was covered in a thick layer of dry dung. Grosman and her associates spent many exhausting days clearing the accumulated dung to reach the layer below, which was yet another stratum of goat dung—from the Byzantine era. Goats were popular back then as well, and goatherds were happy to cram them into such a natural enclosure, but clearly, nobody had taken the effort to sweep up the dung and reuse it as fertilizer.

Just before the archeologists despaired and abandoned the layer of fourth- or fifth-century poop, Grosman decided to try to dig a hole down to the bedrock. At the bottom of the pit right at the end on the bedrock, she made a stunning discovery: a scraper made of flint, typical of the Natufian culture. She needed no further proof. The prehistoric human hand poking out of the same layer showed that this was not just any old cave. This was an ancient burial site.

***

The history of death is at least as complicated as that of life. Academic positions about what prehistoric humans thought about death and the dead themselves, including what to do with them, are complicated and contested. Other living beings— dolphins, ravens, monkeys, and certainly elephants—also mourn the death of members of their groups. Some of them even hold what look like farewell ceremonies. But humans are probably the only species that are aware of death not only when they meet it, but throughout their lives. We live in constant dread of our mortality and have therefore developed rituals for parting from life and parting from the dead.

The oldest cemetery in the world is a pit of bones, discovered in Spain in 1983. It is not exactly a pit, more like a natural hidden shaft created in the karstic rock. At the bottom of the shaft, archeologists discovered the skeletons of at least thirty prehistoric humans dated to 400,000 years ago, and it is hard to believe that they wound up there by accident. Someone placed or threw them there with some sort of intention. Perhaps the intention of burying them.

Nearly twenty years after this pit of bones was discovered, it was found to contain an object that not only strengthened the hypothesis that this was a burial site but also hinted at burial rituals. This object was a hand axe, the trademark tool of *Homo erectus*, the ancestor of the people buried there. It was not just a hand axe, but one made of rare reddish rock, probably for the purpose of being buried with the dead as a kind of votive. If this theory is correct, then this is the oldest known example of funerary art: the beginning of a long tradition of burying items with the dead, the most famous of which are the contents of the pharaohs' tombs in ancient Egypt, the Terracotta Army in the mausoleum of Qin Shi Huang (the first emperor of China), and the presidential seal on the whale's tooth that Jackie Kennedy placed in the grave of her husband, President John F. Kennedy, who had been a collector of ivory paraphernalia.

At the start of the 2010s, in a region of South Africa known as the cradle of humanity because of its dense concentration of prehistoric sites, a cave was discovered and named "Rising Star." Deep in the cave, archeologists uncovered hundreds of bones and teeth from eighteen different individuals. This is the African site with the richest human remains dated to 300,000 years ago. Nothing else was discovered in this cave besides bones and teeth, and the researchers argue that this was a burial site—the second oldest in the world after the pit of bones in Spain.

Much more striking evidence of prehistoric funerary practices has been unearthed in the Qafzeh Cave near Nazareth and the Es-Skhul Cave on Mount Carmel. These are the oldest burial sites in the world containing complete human skeletons, and in humanmade pits (as opposed to natural underground caverns). Each cave was found to contain over ten buried bodies, all classified as archaic *Homo sapiens* and dated to 100,000 years ago. In the Qafzeh Cave, archeologists discovered a child with his left hand placed on the skull of a fallow deer, whose antlers rested on his neck. In the Es-Skhul Cave, they found an adult man next to a pig's jawbone and another adult man next to a cow's head. Some researchers argue that the animals did not end up there by chance but were buried in a meaningful ritual. Others are more hesitant and note that many of these animal remains were found in the caves, so their proximity to the deceased might be a coincidence.

Mary Steiner, an anthropologist from Arizona University and one of the leading researchers in the field of Paleolithic human behavior, argues that these findings represent for the first time in human history a ritual connection between the dead and the living. They clearly reflect grief, she argues, of the sort unknown to us from before, which developed from that point on. Perhaps more importantly, they were also early evidence of social inequality. Certain figures in the group were seen as more special than the others, or maybe even irreplaceable, and their burial in a manner that allowed them to be discovered tens of thousands of years later is proof. It is doubtful whether most people, the "ordinary folk," were afforded such honors. They were probably buried in shallow graves that usually left no traces. Predators start the job, weather damage and floods finish it—and good luck finding any bones from such graves hundreds of thousands of years later.

Daniel Naveh, an Israeli anthropologist who researches the Nayak hunter-gatherer group in southern India, specializes among other things in funeral customs. "Death plays a minor role in their culture," he explains in a conversation about the Nayaka people, "and so the handling of dead bodies is also a minor issue. If someone dies far from the group, they'll leave him there as carrion for the animals in the forest. If he dies in the camp, in most cases they'll lay him down in his hut and bring it down over him. Afterwards, the group will migrate elsewhere, without the bad memories."

Naveh tries to apply the Nayaka people's approach to the deaths of their beloved friends in his own volunteer work, counselling people with terminal illnesses and their families. He tries to encourage them to think of death as natural, as part of life, without the anxieties and fears of the Western mind. According to him, the Nayaka's feelings of grief are authentic and profound but simply different from our own. The day of someone's death is full of emotion and drama, but the bereavement process is short. "Actual graves would be very shallow," Naveh explains graphically, "of the sort a hand could poke out from."

***

It is no coincidence that the fundamental and significant pivot in human history, which was also reflected in burial customs, happened more or less at the same time as the ritual in the Hilazon Cave. This was just as the seeds of the Agricultural Revolution started germinating and hunter-gatherers turned their backs on the lifestyle that had allowed humanity to prosper for generations. They started migrating less and growing more of their own food.

The revolution erupted 15,000 years ago in the region known as the southern Levant, which includes modern-day Syria, Lebanon, Jordan, Israel, and the Sinai Desert. Archeologically, the change was striking: it left its mark in the findings from the innovative culture of this period in Wadi Natuf, east of Israel's international airport. This was the material culture that Dorothy Garrod identified even before starting her monumental project on Mount Carmel. A woman of finely tuned senses, Garrod understood that she had stumbled across something previously unknown, which did not exist in Europe. She was not wrong. Her classification of the Natufian culture as one of "early farmers" remains the prevailing view today.

If we had a time machine that could take us back to this distant period, we would land in a surprising architectural landscape of very small villages, including round buildings, some of which were made of stone. Not the walls, and definitely not the roofs, which were made of fronds, but there was stone in their foundations. We modern humans have taken this business up a notch, building towers that touch the sky. The Natufians were the ones who began it.

The Natufians were also the first people who switched to permanent settlement, living in one place at least for certain parts of the year. This was their major innovation. From the thresholds of their huts, they could witness the different seasons and decide whether it was even worth relocating. They watched fig trees blossom, flower, and bear delicious fruit. In the ongoing argument about why prehistoric humans switched to permanent settlement and food production—the two hallmarks of the Agricultural Revolution—it used to be assumed that people first started producing food and then permanently settled the areas near their blossoming fields. The Natufian culture, however, points in the opposite direction: first people switched to permanent settlement, and only then did they abandon hunting and gathering in favor of food production. "They were farmers," concludes Grosman with a slight cough to disguise her certainty and avoid sparking an academic firestorm. Nevertheless, her opinion is clear: the Natufians were farmers, with fields that she hopes to uncover one day.

In their stone houses the Natufians had large stone tools, pestles and mortars, which they processed plant-based foods with, especially grains. They also had storage areas, such as small granaries. The Natufians were the inventors of the year-round pantry. As long as humans wandered from place to place, they had barely enough possessions to fill a shopping basket. Once we switched to permanent settlements, we started amassing equipment and objects: food, tools, clothes, and more. Now, we have walk-in wardrobes, piles of used sneakers, sheds for screwdrivers and old bicycles, and drawers brimming with cutlery for once-a-year special events. The average American household has no fewer than 300,000 "things," which we as a species started hoarding 12,000 years ago.

Natufian villages have been found to contain sickles, an innovative new technology for systematically harvesting grain. It was not a long leap from sickles to combine harvesters, or from round huts to skyscrapers, and it was certainly shorter than humanity's journey to the sickle. Until then, humans used to eat plants gathered from their surroundings. The Natufians took one, even two steps forward. They harvested grain on an unprecedented scale, and more importantly, they also processed, crushed, and stored it. Plant-based food became an increasingly important component of their diet. They did not become vegetarians, and they still *loved* meat, especially gazelle meat, but it was clearly inadequate on its own, both in terms of quantities and fat content. The distressing decline of megafauna—horses, cattle, and deer—forced them to make adaptations again. Of the sort that would one day appear on our tables as sliced bread and breakfast cereals.

This period also witnessed a burst of creativity, with a range of figurines, engraved stones, and what are usually characterized as artworks. If art exists for communication, then this was an epoch of non-stop discourse. The old order had changed; what was once stable and fixed no longer suited the new reality, and prehistoric comfort zones were abandoned. This was a vibrant new world, and its inhabitants adapted their communications accordingly.

Here we return to burial customs. They too experienced decisive change. "In Natufian [culture]," says Grosman, "there is a supersonic boom around this whole subject." From this point on, it became a common practice for people to bury their dead underground near their places of settlement or within their boundaries.

The numbers were significant: Natufian burial sites are not random discoveries here and there but regular fixtures, facts of life unearthed at every archeological excavation from this period. There are single graves and mass graves, and in many cases, body parts were removed at the time of burial or shortly thereafter. No fewer than twenty-eight people were buried in the Hilazon Cave, mostly chopped up and squished together in shared pits. Only three of them were buried whole and alone. They were all women.

—*Was that a coincidence?*

"Absolutely not," says Grosman.

—*And one of these three women was the one for whom the event that you described earlier was held? She was special.*

"I think that the others were also special women, but yes, one of them was unique. She was the one found with the leopard and eagle remains, a cow's tail, a wild boar's trotter, and ninety tortoise shells."

—*What was she?*

"A shaman."

—*What does that mean, in your understanding?*

"You could think of it as a generic title for spiritual affairs, or you could develop it in the direction of all sorts of examples of shamans around the world. The shaman buried in the cave was hunchbacked, very short, and old. Many 'messed up' people become shamans, because they're special, frightening.

She had powers and the animals were spiritual go-betweens for her. I imagine that all 200 people who came here knew her as someone both scary and important."

***

Let's take a deep breath and set aside everything we think and know about shamans. We need to drop our natural cynicism for just a moment, and preferably also our rationality, and only then can we try to understand the shaman's role in traditional societies—and beyond.

The word "shaman" apparently originates in eastern Siberia, on the Mongolian border, and its meaning in the Manchu-Tungus family of indigenous languages in the region is "one who knows." From there it spread to indigenous societies across Siberia, was exported to Europe, and spread around the world like an anthropological wildfire. There are Aborigine shamans in the Australian outback, shamans in the African savanna, shamans among the Native American tribes, Inuit shamans in the Arctic north, and of course shamans across the Amazon basin. Shamans can even be found in Los Angeles, London, and Paris. The Manchu-Tungus languages may be extinct, but shamans are thriving.

Shamanistic practices and beliefs have intrigued arche-ologists, scholars of religion, historians, philosophers, psych-ologists, and of course very many anthropologists. Dozens of books have been written on the subject, hundreds if not thousands of articles have been published, and there is even a scientific journal dedicated to shamanism. Its popularity is not limited to academia, and any self-respecting travel company offers its customers at least one adventure holiday including an encounter with an authentic shaman.

Shamanism is a system of beliefs and rituals that predated the advent of modern religions and was common, in one way or another, to all indigenous societies in the world. These societies typically believe, as we have already seen, that humans are not alone in the world. There are other important and powerful entities. They, the shamans, are shape-shifting beings that can take the form of animals, plants, ancestors, and so forth.

These entities are responsible for the proper functioning of the world, and when problems emerge, humans must establish contact with the entities and use them to find a solution. The spectrum of problems is wide and diverse: health issues, difficulties finding game to hunt, droughts or ferocious rains, tensions in the family, depression, and listlessness. Ecological troubles are also brought to the attention of these entities if, for example, the forests are not flourishing as they once did, the fruit trees are yielding less, honey has become harder to find, and so on. These are problems that only indigenous societies seem to take seriously.

Shamans are key figures in this system. They are the go-betweens, who liaise between the earthly and the spiritual, between humans and the powers above and beyond them. They are the emissaries to other worlds. They perform this mission mostly by entering fluctuating mental states, created with the help of certain substances. Sometimes a shaman will enter this state without mind-altering substances, but rather thanks to exceptional personal abilities, physical abnormalities (such as those of the woman in the Hilazon Cave) or extreme physiological factors (such as epilepsy). The shaman undergoes a personal metamorphosis, and some researchers claim the transformation is not mental but physical: the shaman enters another body to deal with whatever needs fixing or treating. Some shamans are supposedly all-knowing, and some have specific fields of expertise; some shamans diagnose, others provide treatment. They are healers who impart peace and tranquility and serve as repositories of knowledge. As Grosman explains, shamans operate in a wide range of variables and possibilities.

Davi Kopenawa, a member of the Yanomami people in the Amazon basin on the Brazilian–Venezuelan border, is one of the most famous and influential shamans in Western culture. He is a sought-after speaker at scientific conferences, articulates his positions well on social media, and his book, *The Falling Sky*, offers readers a rare and prescient first-person account of a subject that is usually described in third-person terms. As a child, Kopenawa survived two deadly epidemics that felled thousands of members of his community, introduced by missionaries who entered the heart of the jungle. These church emissaries taught him to read and write and helped him to acquire language skills and a broad education, but their fanaticism and obsessiveness were never to his taste, and after much of his close family died of measles—another gift from the white people—Kopenawa decided to turn his back on the missionaries and save not just his own life but also his spiritual heritage. He returned to his roots, walked for many months through the depths of the jungle of his childhood and, under the guidance of one of his people's elder sages, he learned what he was destined to be: a shaman.

Back then, Kopenawa did not know how to dream properly: "Only an inner grasp in the dreams of the spirits allows the shaman's imagination to move far away. Without this control, one cannot understand the meaning of the sky, the stars, the moon, the thunder, and the rain," he explains in his book. He says that the key, the power of introspection, is acquired through the study and continued drinking of ayahuasca. Not everyone, Kopenawa emphasizes, can consume this plant and experience its full power. This requires living in the right environment. To grow up in the rainforest.

Kopenawa pours his concoction into a hollow cane and blows it into the nostrils of his patients, transferring part of his powers into the other person's consciousness. The spirits of the rainforest or hordes of powerful animals will help him communicate with his patient and understand what hurts them, what bothers them, and whether they can be released from their condition and cured. "We heal people like doctors, but it's not just about health," Kopenawa emphasizes, "We care for the world. And when shamans care for the world, it is possible to live in peace." Nature is part of the healing process, and these activities are undertaken out of concern for the wellbeing not only of the patient but also of their environment.

The drinking of naturally sourced mind-altering substances is a basic and fundamental element of shamanistic activities around the world. The best-known of these substances is ayahuasca, produced from a plant of the same name. Ayahuasca drinking rituals have become a popular trend in the Western world, and participants—including celebrities—speak of out-of-body experiences and visions, sensing a profound connection to the cosmos, and feeling reborn. These are powerful experiences, which is why people are careful to avoid using ayahuasca irresponsibly and sharply distinguish it from other familiar drugs. This is not a substance for getting high or having a wild night out. It offers a physically and emotionally disorienting experience, a journey to other worlds, requiring the oversight and guidance of responsible figures.

In the Arctic and sub-Arctic regions, devoid of trees of any sort, the most common spiritual ritual is known as "shaking tent." This is a profoundly important rite held after dark at the end of summer at family gathering points. Constant, rhythmic drumming plays a core role in inducing participants into a different mental state. The shaman or other presiding figure enters a tent alone and summons the spirits. The participants outside are called in from time to time to ask the questions that unsettle them, and they might hear what the future holds for them or learn about what happened to them in the past.

Adrian Tanner, one of the most fascinating and committed anthropologists we met, presents a thought-provoking position about his personal experiences with shamans in the wastelands of northeastern Canada. "I kept being surprised by them," he says, "especially because they challenged all my automatic assumptions about the spiritual world. Shamanism is anything but a system of closed-minded thought."

In his gripping book, *Bringing Home Animals*, Tanner discusses hunting customs and the deep relationship between hunted animals and the hunters themselves: "Many hunters have different techniques for divining the future, most of which focus on the hunt—where and when they will find and kill game. These same techniques are often used for other purposes."

—*What purposes, for example?*

"Finding a lost object, predicting the arrival of foreigners in the camp, etc.," explains Tanner, as our guest at a conference in Tel Aviv.

—*Can you give an example?*

"Once we waited a few days in a pre-agreed place for the arrival of a trader in a light aircraft. The people shared their dreams about the date of his arrival and also burned Arctic hare bones to predict whether he would show up on that date. Bones are usually used to foretell the results of a hunt and the location of the animals. One might get the impression that whatever entity provides this information—a spirit in a dream or a hare bone—is all-powerful, omniscient. But it turns out that like humans, it is also easily misled and used."

Tanner—whom we met several times in Labrador, Canada—describes the case of a trained and responsible shaman, who nevertheless charged money to perform "shaking tent" rites for tourists. The tent indeed shook, and the visitors received full bang for their buck. After this shaman's death, Tanner asked his widow if the spirits that he summoned into the tent minded being exploited for a profit-seeking enterprise. "Oh, the spirits didn't know about the money," she chirped.

As simple as that: *they didn't know*. Soothsayers, fortune-tellers, and other magicians, serious as they may be, might always have one eye on earthly affairs. This is certainly the case when faced with people who have only come to take a peek and a selfie, and will pay what it takes to shake a tent and arouse the spirits.

***

To be sure that we were not missing anything or excitedly rushing to judgment, we booked a meeting with Dandan Bolotin, a biologist and botanist by training and a devout rationalist who has spent more than six years in the rainforests of northern Ecuador. He arrived in the early 1990s to conduct a comprehensive academic study into medicinal herbs, with U.S. government funding. During his work, Bolotin met no fewer than thirty shamans—men and women—who introduced him to the botanical world that they know and use in their work. He walked for days on end, sailed on the river, and hired light aircraft to take him to every corner of the jungle. He even came across a Yiddish-speaking shaman.

So as not to waste precious time, this Israeli researcher developed a system for ranking the knowledge and quality of each shaman and appealed only to those who had at least three independent referees. One shaman stood out above all: El Paro, from the Quechua people, who became Bolotin's mentor and close friend. It took a long time for El Paro to agree to take the young researcher into the deepest parts of the rainforest, not because he did not trust him but because he was concerned that the guest's scent would disturb the forest spirits. Bolotin, a polite man who diligently uses soap and deodorant every day, was forced to wash with the essence of a plant that smelled foul but was apparently much better suited to the rainforest than his Western aroma.

Like Kopenawa, El Paro had also reached his status through many years of learning under the guidance of a relative and the generous drinking of mind-altering substances. In his case, it was ayahuasca, the main toolkit of most Amazonian shamans. The substance extracted from this plant has no healing or prophetic powers, but it lets shamans know which interventions are needed for the situation at hand.

On one occasion, Bolotin recalls, El Paro was summoned to treat an unconscious man sprawled across the entrance of his hut. The man seemed to be in a serious condition. Bolotin was concerned, and the shaman said that he could not know what to do without going "inside." And by "inside," he meant into the unconscious man's body. That's exactly what El Paro did, with the help of an ayahuasca potion. When he got out, he said that there was nothing to worry about and that the man was healthy. Everything was functioning as required, except that around his heart was there an enchantment that looked like a yellow bullet. "So why didn't you take it out?" Bolotin wondered. "That's not my expertise," explained El Paro.

The shaman sent a boat to collect another shaman, who was an expert in these matters. It took a long time for the second shaman to arrive, equipped with a cloth bag full of plants, during which period the patient was still not moving and was hardly breathing. The second shaman shoved some sort of powder into the unconscious man's nostrils and burned tendrils around his head. The thick, scalding smoke filled the air, and the two shamans spent a few minutes sucking on the region of the man's neck and crotch. About a quarter of an hour later, the man woke up, propped himself up next to the healers, and the three men started chatting as if nothing had happened. Only one person was in total shock: Bolotin, who couldn't believe his eyes.

For a long time, Bolotin refused to drink ayahuasca. He eventually gave in to pressure from the camera team filming his life in the jungle. It was his first time, and according to him, nothing to write home about. Maybe this was because the cameras were trained on him. The second time, however, something incredible and inexplicable happened to him. He felt himself leaving his own body and entering the rainforest in El Paro's footsteps. Headlight beetles flickered all around him and a majestic jaguar prowled out of the trees. In this altered mental state, Bolotin knew that this was one of the typical manifestations of the rainforest goddess. He also remembered that he had not met a jaguar before this journey. He told El Paro, who was next to him, that the goddess had not noticed him, and then the jaguar turned and glared straight at the skeptical researcher. That was enough. Bolotin, drained, marched all the way back to his hammock. But his hammock was occupied: he himself was already lying down in it.

Bolotin tells us this story as he hosts us on his remote farm, at a time when he is preoccupied with such trifles as finding a mechanic to fix his broken-down tractor. No, he has no explanation for this experience: he doesn't believe in the soul, certainly not in spirits and demons, but that astral experience was exactly what happened there. And not just there. El Paro was able to tell Bolotin afterwards about every branch that he had leaned against and where exactly he had slipped by the river. He had been there, on the same trip or journey or whatever you want to call it. "All the shamans I met were responsible for the connection between spiritual entities and the locals," Bolotin says in summary. "They were the conduit to the goddess of the forest, to the mountains, to the jungle, and to the mighty beasts."

Many years before Bolotin's experiential journey to Ecuador, Carlos Castaneda's book *The Teachings of Don Juan* was published in 1968 in the United States. The book, supposedly based on Castaneda's academic fieldwork and encounters with an influential shaman, was translated into many languages and became a global bestseller and a must-read for teenagers. It was discussed in countless social events, and there were bitter arguments about its authenticity. In addition to all this, Castaneda's work prompted the emergence of a movement of spiritual seekers, who wanted to find their own shamans and experience similar experiences to those of the hero of the story. This was undoubtedly one of the bases for New Age culture and the mystical renaissance that gripped the Western world. Soon enough, people discovered that they too could be shamans, or at least call themselves shamans, even if they were born in the suburbs of Cleveland and their parents dreamed of them becoming lawyers.

***

Just before we return to the cars that we left in the dry river valley of Nahal Hilazon and rush back to our grey yet blessed lives, Leore Grosman tells us that there, in the valley, right under the cave, lives a shaman. According to her Facebook page, she is the successor of the shaman buried in the cave 12,000 years ago. Like her, she too uses tortoises to channel her powers. Because of the public health guidelines during the coronavirus pandemic, the tortoise shaman only receives customers by prior appointment and with as much social distancing as possible during her trance.

Hilazon Cave—a view of the excavation, looking out from within the cave

CHAPTER 8

MANIPULATIONS

10,000 years ago

From Jericho to Göbekli Tepe, southeastern Turkey

**Who built a monumental tower at the lowest place on earth?
Who appeared to hold the sun in the palm of his hand?
Why might we envy modern-day hunter-gatherers? And was
the Agricultural Revolution really *that* revolutionary?**

It looked like the famous pictures of dockyards or coal mines
during the Great Depression. Men in their work clothes
huddling every morning near the gates, praying for the duty
manager to relieve their despair and the indignity of hunger.
The oppressive desert heat and the penury of the refugee camps
with their densely packed mud huts formed the backdrop for
the excavations at Tel Jericho in the early 1950s. In front of the
crowds of jobseekers stood a middle-aged British woman: a
stern character with a sturdy physique, thinning hair, blue eyes,
and "a cigarette ever-present in her nicotine-stained hand," as
she is described in her biography.

The woman carefully selected her laborers, who tiptoed
around her and addressed her as *set*, "madam" in Arabic. Her
colleagues and acquaintances called her Kay and treated her as
respectfully as her day laborers did. She was the *grande dame* of
twentieth-century biblical archeology. Her name was Kathleen
Kenyon, and the excavations she oversaw with such gusto
and supreme professionalism made Tel Jericho a landmark in
human history and one of the most significant archeological
discoveries of the twentieth century.

Kenyon's father was the director of the British Museum, a byword for some of the most important, if not *the* most important, historic and prehistoric collections in the world. His daughter's path into the world of archeology was therefore paved from birth. She began her meteoric career in Southern Rhodesia (modern-day Zimbabwe), where she found the remains of magnificent structures attributed—erroneously of course—to the Queen of Sheba. This was an all-female expedition, which was no easy matter for the local workers, and produced some surprising conclusions. European experts, including Kenyon, put little stock in the abilities of Africans, but the findings there proved beyond doubt that these breathtaking structures were built by the locals' distant ancestors. Kenyon displayed the traits that would define her whole career, especially in Jericho: exclusive loyalty to the archeological record rather than to prior assumptions or to benefactors.

At the next excavation project—in St Albans, north of London—Kenyon was introduced to Sir Mortimer Wheeler, and together they developed a scientific method that became the gold standard at archeological sites worldwide: the Wheeler–Kenyon method. Until then, archeologists had dug random exploratory trenches up and down their sites, but this quick and sweeping method was ruinous for the treasures buried underground. Wheeler and Kenyon took an almost diametrically opposed approach: they opened up one 5m² (54ft²) grid at a time and meticulously peeled back the archeological layers one by one in chronologically descending order, from the most recent to the oldest. The flanks of each excavated square grid were left untouched, allowing the archeologists to control the dig and document each stratum with precision.

Kenyon never married, and her three great loves were archeology, dogs, and gin. In what little spare time she had, she wrote hundreds of essays and letters. Many of them were sharply critical of the Zionist movement and championed the Arab side in their conflict over a narrow strip of land. A land whose scientific treasures were the envy of dozens of archeologists from different countries and areas of expertise, who wanted mainly to unearth sites from the Bible. The ancient city of Jericho and its walls were the jewels in this crown, and Kenyon was given the honor of trying to salvage it from the sands of time.

This was not the first excavation in Jericho. Charles Warren had dug there in the mid-nineteenth century, but he had little clue what to do at this complicated site. John Garstant, the head of Mandatory Palestine's Antiquities Department, oversaw a long excavation at ancient Jericho and was the first to understand that this was a multi-layered tel, or archeological mound, with one period on top of the other—but he failed to find what he and many others were truly after: evidence supporting the biblical narrative. That was what Kenyon was supposed to do when she reached the lowest place on earth, knowing better than anyone else in her profession what and how to dig there. She had already accumulated rich experience from biblical-era archeological excavations, including in Samaria, and her mission was quite elementary: to identify the walls that Joshua brought down when the Israelites began their conquest of the Promised Land and to date them. And if possible, also to find remains of the trumpets that brought the walls down.

Kathleen Kenyon did not find the rubble of Jericho's walls, and she definitely didn't find any biblical trumpets. What began as two archeological seasons expanded into seven and demonstrated that the story in the book of Joshua was probably utter fiction. Or at least, that if it happened, it definitely wasn't in Jericho. In the Late Bronze Age (1500–1200 BCE), when the Israelites supposedly conquered this land, Jericho was not even inhabited. The place was deserted, like other sites mentioned in the same biblical tale. Kenyon did, however, unearth one of the oldest permanent settlements in the world.

It was a big village, not quite a town, over 9,000 years old, surrounded by stone walls, on top of which stood an 8m-high (26ft) tower. This is without a doubt the earliest monumental building known to modern scholarship. The world's first skyscraper. There is nothing else like it, not even close. It was a bit like the discovery of the futuristic DeLorean in the garage in the first instalment of the *Back to the Future* trilogy. Where had it come from?

The archeologists thought that it was a watchtower, a familiar part of fortifications from much later periods. But at the time it was built, there was nobody and nothing that Jericho's inhabitants needed protecting from. There were no foreign armies—there were no armies at all—and nobody could threaten the sort of invasion that would have to be fended off with such defenses. Until just a few minutes previously, humans were still wandering around, hunting, gathering, and at most building seasonal huts—so where on earth did these walls and the three-story-high tower come from?

Maybe ancient Jericho's walls were designed to protect against floods? This was one of the hypotheses that were floated, and there was a certain logic to it given the importance of the agricultural fields and the flash floods that gush off the desert cliffs into the gorges. But this explanation could not hold water. At any rate, this watchtower would have been ineffective against a sudden desert tsunami. There were other practical explanations (and no doubt, more will be offered), but it is important to remember that the people who built this tower had probably never seen a tower before, had no idea what a tower was, and were definitely not thinking about how it might protect them against freak dangers that probably didn't exist.

The reason for this monumental construction is probably best understood not from a contemporary practical perspective, but as an impressive expression of the prehistoric Zeitgeist. The spirit of the most dynamic and perhaps dramatic prehistoric era: the Neolithic (the New Stone Age), best known for the so-called Neolithic Revolution—or Agricultural Revolution.

The Agricultural Revolution, and even the Neolithic period, will sound more familiar to most ears than such strange and obtuse terms as "Acheulean culture," "Mousterian," "Natufian," and "Lower and Upper Paleolithic." Some might even associate it with the decisive transition toward permanent settlement, the construction of real houses, the beginning of agriculture, and the domestication of plants and livestock. In other words: this was the revolution that determined our fate and was nothing less than the dawn of civilization.

That's certainly how the Agricultural Revolution is imagined, but we cannot be sure that such a revolution ever took place. Modern research is divided on the exact nature of this "revolution": was it an event or a process? What was the reason, or what were the reasons, for this dramatic change? Did people rapidly adopt a bundle of changes—of which agriculture was just one—or did the revolution begin much earlier, and was the Neolithic, around 10,000 years ago, just its most pronounced phase? As we recall, back at the descent from the Hilazon Cave we reasoned that its denizens were farmers who lived in stone houses, and this was a few thousand years before the Neolithic Revolution. This would have made the Agricultural Revolution a protracted process, not a bona fide revolution like the Industrial Revolution, for example, which unfolded over the space of a mere 100 years.

In any case, there is one thing that everyone agrees on: this chapter in the prehistory of humanity is best described starting here, at Tel Jericho.

***

Using the grid method to excavate archeological layers in descending order, Kenyon and her dozens of laborers made their way through several distinct layers of the Neolithic period. These layers represented thousands of years of human existence, during which at least one big thing remained the same: people built houses and stayed put. Year by year, generation by generation. This was no trifling matter. This was a new and totally different phenomenon. Prehistoric humans moved from place to place, crossing continents and sometimes looping back to familiar sites, from tranquil lakes to protective caves. At a later stage, as we saw in the previous chapter, they even briefly lived in huts with stone foundations. But they did not lay these foundations, nor did they build walls and roofs, and they certainly did not bury their dead under their flagstone floors.

The different stages in Neolithic Jericho could be discerned from variations in the nature of the settlement, its size, and its economy. Yet across all these stages, a new human enterprise appeared, like at other Neolithic sites in the world: the increased exploitation of the environment—that is, the intensified use of plants, stones, trees, and everything else that was once simply part of nature. One unmistakable hallmark of this era was the axe—like one you might buy in a hardware store, just made of stone. This was a remarkably effective tool for chopping down trees, a task that would become increasingly intensive and would transform the landscape and the world's forests long before the invention of the electric saw. The prevalence of the axe and permanent housing represented a prehistoric drama: humanity's unprecedented exploitation of Mother Earth.

The quest to understand the reasons for the transition from a nomadic existence to a sedentary lifestyle and agriculture has given rise to a plethora of explanations and theories. By and large, the argument divides into two sets of people. In one corner are those who believe that this was a conscious and deliberate process that took place independently in different places around the world as a result of similar human needs and abilities. In the other are those who think that this was a circumstantial event, the result of an external force operating on humanity—an invisible hand, driven by a combination of factors.

Back in the 1920s and 1930s, the influential Australian archeologist V. Gordon Childe presented a model known as the Oasis Theory. According to this model, climate change and a precipitous drop in precipitation forced humanity to become concentrated in several fertile valleys and to sustain itself collectively through agriculture. This was a classic Marxist theory, which viewed the control of the means of production as the main engine of change in history. Another theory was proposed by Lewis Binford, the researcher who tore to shreds the theory of an "elephant massacre" at Torralba in Spain (see page 25). In this debate, Binford attributed the transition to agriculture to the thawing of the glaciers, which limited the areas available for human habitation but also created water-rich areas suitable for intensive agriculture. These are two examples of one kind of circumstantial approach: the argument that these changes were propelled by necessity and the opportunities to which they gave rise.

Another circumstantial approach holds that the changes were driven by a purely accidental process. This is the dump-heap hypothesis. In this theory, naturally fertile "ecological niches" emerged in different parts of the world. These were places where humans domesticated animals, dumped their garbage, relieved themselves, and so forth. According to this model, certain plants took advantage of this situation and effectively "domesticated" and improved themselves: they flourished, spread, grew roots, and yielded more fruit than wild plants. Humans were enthralled by what they saw, fell into these plants' honey trap, and started systematically sustaining a phenomenon that began as an evolutionary diversion, growing out of local landfills.

Many reasonable and responsible researchers lose their cool when presented with ideas like these. Accidental? Circumstantial? Honey trap? In their view, based on the archeological evidence and deep botanical and zoological knowledge, the domestication of flora and fauna was anything but an accident. This was a deliberate, conscious process undertaken by people with a keen understanding of the nuances of their surroundings. People who could tell apart different kinds and species of plants and trees, who learned which of the many varieties of cereals, peas, and chickpeas were worth domesticating and which were not. In this account, Neolithic humans knew what they were doing and why. They simply never imagined that, one day, their manipulation of nature, the innocent yet sophisticated domestication of cereals and legumes, would be seen as having locked the gates of paradise behind humankind.

While advocates of the theories of compulsion and coincidence note the possible factors behind changes in human behavior, those who favor theories of conscious choice fail to propose driving forces of their own. Even if we agree that humans possessed a deep familiarity with the world around them and a significant ability to manipulate it, why did they decide to start when they did? Why not tens of thousands of years earlier, or a few thousand years later? The reasons for the timing and the catalyst for change remain a mystery.

The debate about this issue, which has been raging for nearly a century, will surely continue to preoccupy scholars, each according to their worldview. Yet a question that is no less interesting than "how did this happen?" is *why did they agree?*" Why did hunter-gatherers turn their backs on a lifestyle that had proven its worth over hundreds of thousands of years and choose—if they had a choice—to walk in completely the opposite direction? Why did they abandon their familiar lives and take what was for them a fairly reckless bet? What might seem obvious to us—Western individuals, accustomed to a life of comfort, fully stocked supermarket shelves, and delivery services from nearby pizzerias—is not necessarily the perfect model for a good life. Over the past decade of the twenty-first century, we have already seen widespread personal and collective disillusionment about the wellbeing promised by progress. Nevertheless, we tend to assume that for all our difficulties, we are much better off than hunter-gatherers, past and present.

In a ground-breaking article titled "The Worst Mistake in Human History," Jared Diamond examines this assumption and presents conflicting data from modern-day hunter-gatherer groups. "It turns out," writes Diamond, "that these people have plenty of leisure time, sleep a good deal, and work less hard than their farming neighbors." The Bushmen in the Kalahari Desert work less than twenty hours a week to sustain themselves, the Hazda nomads of Tanzania make do with a fourteen-hour working week, and neither group has to worry about mortgages or credit ratings. They live quite well. It's just like in the well-known story, with a dozen different versions, about the American who visits an exotic island and sees a native islander swinging in a hammock between two coconut trees. The tourist asks the man why he is content with the one coconut in his hands instead of expanding his operations, picking more off the tree, selling them and growing his business until one day he can retire to an exotic location and spend all day in the shade of a coconut tree. "But that's what I'm doing now," says the local man to the tourist. Point made. Agriculture was a problematic, difficult, and even dangerous enterprise. The harvests depended on the grace of the heavens, and swarms of parasites could eradicate whole fields farmers had labored over. "It's almost inconceivable that Bushmen, who eat 75 or so wild plants, could die of starvation the way hundreds of thousands of Irish farmers and their families did during the potato famine of the 1840s," writes Diamond.

Agricultural work also requires many working hands for plowing, sowing, and harvesting. You wake up early in the morning and when the sun sets, you're still in the field. Naturally and unavoidably, small groups merge and grow bigger and denser. The density gives rise to other problems: pollution, disease, and quarrels with the neighbors. And all this—the grueling work, the limited diet, the dangers of famine and overcrowding—was just a preview of the fearsome monster that lay beyond the verdant hills: the emergence of a ruling class. Those who controlled the flow of wealth, or the whole of a society's reserves; those who told others what to do and were obeyed; the powerful ones. Those because of whom, or for whose sake, the monumental tower was probably built in Jericho some 10,000 years ago.

***

You have to jump through several bureaucratic hoops to get to see the tower up close, certainly if you have Israeli citizenship. You leave Damascus Gate on the northern side of the Old City of Jerusalem and pass several checkpoints on the descent to the

Dead Sea. It's best to make plans with a local fixer to wait for you at a pre-arranged place, and don't forget high-factor sunscreen, because in the summer it will feel like you've reached a place where the ozone layer is an unfounded rumor. It's hot in Jericho. Boiling hot. Considering the weather and heat stress, it would undoubtedly have been better to have visited back when the tower was built, just at the end of the last Ice Age. It would have probably also been less hassle.

The key to understanding the reason for the tower's existence is its location in the topography of the Jordan Valley. Long before you reach the tower, something else stands out: the Mount of Temptation, a sharp peak above the desert cliffs that seem to close off and frame the fertile Jericho Valley.

The mountain is unmissable. Jesus spent forty days and nights there, according to Christian tradition, resisting the Devil's temptations; the Hasmoneans, the independent Jewish royal dynasty, built a palace fortress at the top; and the Palestinian Authority takes pride in the national cable car that takes tourists to a look-out point over a stunning vista. The Mount of Temptation was also there 10,000 years ago. Anyone who climbed up the tower's inner stairwell before stepping into the light would have seen the mountain in front of them. It was a humanmade monument in response to a natural wonder.

Unlike in more modern defensive walls, where towers are part of the wall, things were different in Neolithic Jericho. The tower was on the interior of the wall: inside the village. Not only that, but in ancient Jericho, the tower was effectively just the cover. What truly mattered lay inside it: a massive spiral stairwell, leading all the way up to the exit. In other words, this was not a tower with a staircase, but a staircase with its own tower. Moreover, this was the only tower; there were no others along the wall. The tower and the wall emulate the primal wilderness in front of them: the tower, the tip of the mountain; the wall, the desert cliffs.

The location of the tower and the stairwell was carefully selected. Roy Liran, an architect who has examined the engineering and environmental aspects of the tower, demonstrates that the diagonal angle of the stairwell exactly matches the angle of the sunset behind the Mount of Temptation during the summer solstice. An azimuth of 290° connects the tower, the mountain, and the setting sun. The sunset in the Judean Desert is truly majestic, even without such constructions. The color of the sky changes, the mountains are painted red, and silence grips the land. Anyone who stood in this Neolithic village on the longest day of the year was surely treated to a powerful, hypnotic, and overwhelming visual display. The shadow of the setting sun in the west would have gradually crept toward the ancient village, subsuming the mountain and the tower into a single dark expanse, growing until the whole desert was consumed in darkness. Anyone who climbed the stairs to the top of the tower would have appeared to be cupping the sun in their hands. This was not just an impressive spectacle, but a scary one. Controlling the masses, 101.

Sunrise and sunset were extremely significant events in the lives of prehistoric humans, as the main way of understanding the rhythm of the seasons and the natural cycle. Things must have been this way since the dawn of humanity (and even today, sunrise and sunset serve as more than tourist attractions and romantic moments). There, in Jericho, humans claimed mastery of the heavenly forces for the first time and brought them down to earth. Into their houses and into their lives. This pattern would repeat itself in other places across the world, which we shall reach at the end of our journey. From Stonehenge in England to the Maya pyramids in Central America and the pharaohs' pyramids in Egypt. These were all enormous monuments built to mark the rising and setting of the sun.

Let's take a few steps back. Jacques Cauvin, a French archeologist who specializes in the prehistory of the Levant, presents an original and thought-provoking approach to the Neolithic Revolution in his book *The Birth of the Gods and the Origins of Agriculture*. Its bottom line is that the use of symbols to influence people's understanding of the world predated the transition from hunting and gathering to agriculture—and paved the way there. First humans invented deities; only then did they domesticate animals, legumes, and cereals.

Cauvin contends that historical forces are often rooted in the human imagination. In his research, therefore, he looks not for grains of wheat or mutations in varieties of lentils, but for evidence of changes in the human imagination. These appeared in the Levant as far back as the Natufian culture, around 1,000 years before the Neolithic Revolution. The representations of animals that we have already seen (see Chapter 6)—such as in the caves of the Dordogne Valley—were devoid of any hierarchy. Mammoths were mammoths; bison were bison. This changed in the tenth century BCE, when there appeared a deity in the shape of a bull alongside a goddess of fertility in the shape of a woman. The human imagination began to distinguish between up and down, between divine forces and daily human existence. This was a psychological change, a change of mindset. A "psycho-cultural revolution," as Cauvin puts it.

Thousands of miles from Jericho, at the Neolithic site of Göbekli Tepe in southeastern Turkey, archeologists since the end of the twentieth century have been unearthing monuments that are no less extraordinary. These are enormous stone circles, at the center of which are giant T-shaped pillars, adorned with a plethora of images from the natural world: aurochs, wild boars, lions, snakes, scorpions, birds of prey, and even a duckling. Some of the animals are endowed with prominent sexual organs, and so are some of the human characters. The pillars themselves seem to be shaped like giant humans, with arms on their sides and belts around their waists. The findings at Göbekli Tepe date to the same period as the earliest Neolithic layer at Jericho. At these two far-flung sites, humans built significant Neolithic centers around huge stone monuments, which remained major attractions for millennia. Both sites, the T-shaped pillars and the tower, are from the tenth century BCE—before the earliest known domestication of plants and animals in the Levant and modern-day Turkey.

The builders of the Göbekli Tepe monuments were hunter-gatherers. They were in transition, on their way to becoming something else, but they still hunted and gathered to earn their keep. They did not come to this site for economic reasons. On the contrary, they arrived for ritual, symbolic, and perhaps even religious reasons. Some consider Göbekli Tepe to be the first temple, the place where the first institutionalized religion was founded. A Neolithic religion. The Turkish government is working hard to promote this branding, marketing the site as the birthplace of the three monotheistic religions. Maybe, just maybe. What's clear is that more and more people converged on this site thousands of years ago. Some of them visited and moved on; others stayed and settled down. First, they domesticated themselves; only then did they domesticate their habitat.

"The Neolithic Revolution," wrote Cauvin in the conclusion of his thought-provoking book, "is a clear demonstration of the fact that man could not completely transform the way he exploited his natural environment, his own settlements, as much as his means of subsistence, without showing at the same time a different conception of the world and himself in that world." Cauvin was aware that his approach was highly unorthodox and cut against the grain of conventional wisdom. Not only were its conclusions radical, but so was his quest for answers in the human soul, rather than in physical remains. Tragically for him, in 2001, shortly after his book was translated into English, he had a stroke and never recovered.

The translator of the English edition, the Scottish archeologist Trevor Watkins, continued Cauvin's work and took it upon himself to defend his positions from academic criticism. We spoke on Zoom to explore whether the ideas in *The Birth of the Gods and the Origins of Agriculture* are still salient.

"Not necessarily," says Watkins in a soft but authoritative and knowledgeable voice. "Nowadays we know that humans were working the land long before domestication, long before there was 'agriculture.' Settled agriculture developed over a very long period. There are studies that show that as far back as the Upper [later] Paleolithic, people were manipulating plants. The birth of agriculture is an erroneous idea. Agriculture wasn't 'born,' it has a long history, from long before domestication."

—*If so, maybe it's also a mistake to speak of a "revolution"?*

"I still use the word 'revolution.' At the end of the Paleolithic era, into the early stages of the Neolithic, we can see a change in the pace of development. Things speed up. Social changes, societal evolution, and cultural changes all happen much faster. Most critically, from my perspective, population sizes also change. From groups of ten, twenty, maybe thirty hunter-gatherers, once they switched to permanent settlement, as soon as they built houses, once everyone built houses, the numbers soared. They more than doubled in size. In Jericho, there were a few hundred people, 700–800, right?"

These were indeed the numbers, more or less, and Neolithic Jericho could undoubtedly take pride in having spearheaded a prehistoric house-building project. In Watkins's view, what made this period so revolutionary had nothing to do with grain or sheep, but houses. These new structures with solid floors, walls, doors, and maybe even windows. Permanent housing.

The long excavations that Watkins conducted at Qermez-Dere in northern Iraq (halted by Saddam Hussein's invasion of Kuwait) gave him evidence and insights into the importance of Neolithic houses. "The home is an architectural expression of an idea. We could tell that houses had been built over and over again at exactly the same spots. They removed the roof, knocked down the building, and then rebuilt it. As if the house itself were buried and rose from the dead. A house has a life. It is not just a shelter, it is full of symbolic activity."

Ian Hodder, the contemporary scholar most associated with the Neolithic, concurs with Watkins. Hodder has been overseeing the excavations at the Neolithic site of Çatalhöyük in central Turkey for twenty-five seasons, and he wrote at the start of his work there that "it seems possible to argue that the process of domestication—the control of the wild—is a metaphor and mechanism for the control of society."

One key factor in understanding the assimilation of change into such a dramatically different lifestyle is the home. "As a metaphor, the idea of the domus used existing fears and emotions to create the channel for structural change," writes Hodder. The longing for one's home, he says, is both a symbol and a means of controlling other people.

Just before joining his family for a hike in the Scottish Highlands, Watkins tells us about a televised experiment broadcast many years ago, in which people had to get by in a Bronze Age village. "Boy, was it difficult!" he recalls, as if he himself were there. Of course, he only watched it on TV, but it was enough to convince him of the caliber of the people he was studying.

"In a relatively short period," he explains, "small groups with informal membership became settled communities with thousands of people living together. They had autonomy. Without police, without judges, they solved their own problems by themselves and lived together according to their own laws, or whatever they were. This went on for hundreds of years, with great success, and in Jericho, it went on for thousands of years. If you ask me, the transition to large, settled communities and the networks of relationships formed between autonomous communities were their greatest achievements. They were fantastic social achievements. And they did this all peacefully, without conflict. That was the revolution. They laid the groundwork for everything that came after them. From this point on, they gave rise to cities, kingdoms, and civilization."

***

In the earliest layers of Tel Jericho, Kathleen Kenyon unearthed a dense cluster of round houses. Next to these houses were storage units, used as granaries or larders. The natural world was generous to the ancient residents of Jericho. Water flowed in abundance and wild plants bloomed in the valleys. They had plenty to collect and store. There is still no evidence of agricultural domestication from this period, but the social changes are striking.

Underneath some of these round houses, Kenyon discovered human skulls. Someone had buried them there, under the floor of their home. This was another novelty, unknown from any previous eras. In the Natufian culture, the number of burials skyrocketed compared to earlier periods. In Neolithic Jericho, the burials entered the village, into people's homes, under their floors. This was a clear statement of continuity, of affinity with their founding fathers and with the place where they lived and would continue to live their lives.

There's no doubt, something had changed. The question is *what*. What happened? Or at least, what probably happened? What happened 10,000 years ago that turned the wheels of revolution at exactly that point or greatly accelerated a process that had started earlier? The answer, once more, may have to do with the decline of humans' long-time friends: the great mammals.

Human beings' dependence on megafauna was a recurring motif of their prehistory. This is an explanation that we keep bumping into: the disappearance of prehistoric elephants 400,000 years ago prompted technological, social, and later physiological changes among *Homo erectus*. The transcontinental extinction of mammoths and woolly rhinoceroses in Europe, and prehistoric horses and wild cattle in other places, 40,000 years ago must be connected to the parallel disappearance of the Neanderthals. Those who remained—that's us—learned to rely on animals of diminishing size, mostly gazelles and deer. Whereas a prehistoric elephant weighed around ten tons and a prehistoric horse or cow weighed a few hundred kilos, the average gazelle weighed just 25kg (55lb). It's almost impolite to compare what used to exist to what remained. And the existence of even these scraggly and lean animals was not guaranteed forever.

In the Natufian culture, people almost exclusively hunted gazelles for food. They also ate many other small, even tiny creatures: tortoises, birds, hares, and snakes. These were always part of the human diet, but as the megafauna population was depleted, these small delicacies featured more prominently on the menu. The same was true of plant-based foods. The discovery of pestles and mortars points to the preparation of flour from wild grains. Early humans sensed the dangers lurking around the corner and found alternatives. Not particularly tasty or satisfying ones, but at least something to serve for dinner.

It's quite possible that humans understood that they too had contributed to the shortages. They were guilty of overhunting and being inconsiderate of their fellow creatures' need to repopulate. Their faith in eternal abundance was broken, even shattered, and this crisis might have been the catalyst for their faith in something new. Someone only needed to exploit the situation and persuade everyone else to take up the gauntlet: to select the right wild plants, commit to working in the fields, ensure a supply of water, build animal enclosures, and so forth. The same somebody (or somebodies) needed to persuade others to jettison a worldview based on reciprocity with nature in favor of one based on exploitation: of nature— and of fellow humans. Manipulative characters definitely existed long before, but as long as everything worked like clockwork they stood no chance. Yet now in the Neolithic, as nature's clockwork became stuck, this was the opportunists' opportunity.

There was enormous pressure to prevent anything else from going haywire, and someone had to promise that the natural cycle would continue. This somebody probably appealed to familiar natural forces and the heavens. A connection with the sun was essential. The stairwell in the tower at Jericho connected the village to the sun; and it connected the village's leaders— those who climbed the stairs—to the force that controlled the cycles of nature: divinity. The mediators between this world and other worlds had used to be the shamans, whose assistance people sought only in times of need, and who were not full-time leaders. But now there appeared a new sort of intermediary, who claimed an exclusive connection with other worlds. These people would soon start giving out orders. And everyone else would have no option but to obey.

A plastered human skull from the Neolithic layer at Jericho

CHAPTER 9

UPSTAIRS DOWNSTAIRS

7,500–6,000 years ago

From the Timna copper mines near the Red Sea to early
"chiefdoms" in Denmark and the Andes in Peru

What did hi-tech look like in the ancient world?
What dramatic prehistoric discoveries were revealed
by the legend of the revolt against the Romans?
What links copper production and social inequality?
And when did we start eating too much sugar?

It all happened because of a bet for five shillings between the English novelist Sir Henry Rider Haggard and his younger brother, who claimed that Sir Henry could not write an adventure book as successful as Robert Louis Stevenson's *Treasure Island.* Sir Henry took up the gauntlet, and within a short time (under two months, according to one version) he handed his publisher the manuscript of *King Solomon's Mines.* The story was about an explorer by the name of Alan Quartermain who tries to discover the biblical king's long-lost gold mines in the heart of Africa. Published in 1885, the book earned Sir Henry much more than his five-shilling bet with his brother. He even coined a dubious phrase that somehow became an established fact: "King Solomon's Mines."

King Solomon did not—as far as anyone knows—have mines of any sort. Certainly not gold or diamond mines, and definitely not in the heart of Africa. The Bible contains no mention of this. What the Bible does contain is plentiful references to the widespread use of copper in the temple that Solomon built.

This inspired archeologists and intrepid explorers to try to track down the sources of this precious metal. Israel's southern Arava Valley, which has a high concentration of metallic rock, was an obvious target for this quest.

Nelson Glueck, an American Jewish archeologist, was the first researcher to connect the findings around Timna in the Arava Valley to the wise king of the Bible and to the tenth century BCE, the hypothesized period of his reign. But when Glueck reached Timna in 1934, what he discovered was not mines but piles of copper slag, a by-product of copper extraction by smelting. The man who uncovered the mines themselves and established the importance of the world of metal in historical research was Glueck's photographer: Beno Rothenberg, the Indiana Jones of local archeology.

Rothenberg, a native of Frankfurt, Germany, was a straight-A student in mathematics and philosophy, a talented photographer, a sensitive poet, a self-taught archeologist, and an adventurer in his soul. He documented the early years of the State of Israel's independence with his camera and was considered one of the standout photographers of its war of independence. Rothenberg learned from the legendary photographer Robert Capa, one of his mentors, that if his photos were not good enough, it meant he was not close enough to the action. He always stuck close, keeping his lens within rifle-range or closer.

Rothenberg photographed the bravery of Israeli soldiers in the battlefield and he took pictures of draft-dodgers in the cities; he recorded humanitarian gestures toward the enemy; and he snapped the difficult scenes of Arabs being expelled from their villages. His loyalties were to the complexities of the world around him, not necessarily to the Zionist ethos, but none of this stopped him from being the favorite photographer of the leaders and generals of the Jewish state-in-the-making.

A newspaper article published after Rothenberg's death at the age of ninety-eight features a picture of him armed with a camera during the Suez Campaign of 1956. He is seen wearing Oxford shoes, thin woolen socks pulled up to his knees, a beret on his head, sunglasses of the sort still considered stylish, and a leopardskin kerchief. It doesn't get more chic than that. He had many lovers: three wives and another partner, Judith Gavish, whom he met during research at the Timna mines. He was sixty years old at the time; she was a twenty-seven-year-old student joining the excavations as a volunteer. They were together until the day he died.

Rothenberg studied archeology on his feet, on long treks across the desert and as an in-house photographer on research expeditions such as Glueck's in Timna. In the introduction to his stunning photography book *God's Wilderness: Discoveries in Sinai*, about his travels in the desert peninsula, the scholarly adventurer wrote: "The Bible was my faithful companion on all my Sinai travels, but on more than one occasion my camera came into conflict with it. I found myself compelled to adjust my preconceived notions of the country to the evidence of my viewfinder."

Broadly speaking, this was also Rothenberg's job as an archeologist: to adjust preconceived notions. His rich accumulated knowledge, original thinking, and his abundant charisma allowed this tall photographer to move to the other side of the lens and, starting in 1959 in the southern Arava Valley, to manage a radically new kind of archeological excavation—an interdisciplinary expedition, with geologists, chemists, and geomorphologists.

Nowadays, nobody loads a pick-up truck with digging equipment and sets out into the field without at least uttering the word "interdisciplinary." But sixty years ago, Rothenberg understood that this was the key to understanding ancient metallurgy. It takes a geologist to interpret the distribution and structure of the layers where copper deposits are buried; a chemist to explain the preconditions for melting certain materials and whether they could be met at the site; a geomorphologist to describe the changes in the natural landscape over time; a physical anthropologist to analyse human remains, if discovered; and so forth. Contrary to Rothenberg's assessment and the tourist pamphlets handed out at the entrance to the site today, this was not the oldest copper mine in the world, but only *one* of the oldest. Yet at Timna, humans undoubtedly laid the foundations for a new field of research: archeometallurgy or the study of metal production technologies, their use, and their role in ancient human societies.

***

The use of metal represents a new chapter in human history, which began in the sixth century BCE: a few thousand years after the Neolithic Revolution (and a very long time before King Solomon). This did not happen by chance, and it is quite clear and agreed upon where it started.

It was no coincidence, because nobody wakes up one morning next to a campfire and discovers to his surprise that the rocks inside have melted and turned into metal. It doesn't work like that. So, it was no more likely than other significant changes, such as the domestication of plants and animals—as we saw in previous chapters—to have been an accident. The process of turning ore—rock that contains metallic minerals—into a liquid metal requires knowledge and tried-and-tested methods. Open campfires will not do the job. Metalsmiths must work with higher temperatures of over 1,000°, with control over the amount of oxygen fed into the flames. In other words, this business was conceived in the minds of prehistoric innovators in ancient research and development units—a hi-tech industry to all intents and purposes.

The birthplace of metalworks, according to the conventional view, was in the Zagros-Taurus Mountains, in modern-day Iran and Turkey. This is a region that still contains rare reserves of native copper in natural chunks of metal. Its presence and discovery probably excited curiosity and a desire to extract similar materials from rocks containing streaks of copper. And that's what people did, with the help of "crucibles"—small, closed, and mobile pot-shaped instruments, inside which they could generate extremely high temperatures. This technological knowledge spread rapidly, as all knowledge does, and within a few hundred years, it had traveled from central Anatolia to the southern Levant; from the first melting crucibles to the Timna copper reserves and Wadi Feynan in the Transjordan.

Erez Ben-Yosef, an archeologist who specializes in metallurgy and took over the research at Timna in 2009, reminds us that two inventions predated the "Metal Revolution" and made it possible: lime production as the basis of plaster and the ceramics industry. These two enterprises were born out of an understanding that materials change qualities under intense heat and can be used to make wonderful things when they come out of the oven. Surprising as it may sound, the first use of metal—unlike most, if not all, technological innovations beforehand—was not driven by a utilitarian calculus. The first metalsmiths were not looking for ways to make arrowheads more lethal or axes more effective. The tools that they made had no practical use. They had another purpose.

"This was not a technological revolution," explains Ben-Yosef in his modest and cramped office at Tel Aviv University. "It had to do with new ideas, with culture, with symbols. In the beginning, metallurgy served social purposes, through worship and rituals. It was the fact that the product had no practical purpose that turned the advent of metal into something extremely significant."

The copper tools forged in Israel over 6,000 years ago, during the Chalcolithic period (the Stone and Copper Age, from *chalkos*, the Greek for "copper"), are breathtakingly beautiful. They are intricate, delicate, and shiny. They were created using a method known as lost-wax casting, based on a beeswax mold surrounded by a solid material (silt). The beeswax melts in the heat, and a complex copper alloy fills the void. After the metallic material cools down and solidifies, all that remains is to dismantle the solid exterior and marvel at the perfectly shaped copper instrument inside. This not only *sounds* complicated; it really *is* complicated to carry out. Nevertheless, it is such a successful method that sculptors and artists still use it today. Simple, cheap, and although modern materials have replaced beeswax, the method is the same.

Moreover, for copper to solidify as required in the mold, it had to be alloyed with other metals, such as arsenic. Ancient metalsmiths knew how to do this as well, and God only knows how they managed to import arsenic all the way from the nearest source in the central Caucasus, hundreds of miles away from the southern Arava. Whenever people in the Chalcolithic period made the effort of casting something that looked like a work tool, such as an axe, it was made in an open mold using pure copper, and was therefore malleable and non-functional. It was a symbolic representation of an axe, using an extraordinary new material.

The most surprising fact of all about copper production in this period is that dozens of miles separated the mines and the manufacturing sites. People mined copper at Timna or northeast of it in Wadi Feynan, loaded heavy blocks of ore onto donkeys, led them to the Beersheba Valley or even further north, and only there did they smelt the ore in unique furnaces—a local industrial upgrade of crucibles—and cast axes and adzes (hoe-like instruments used mainly for woodwork), and maybe also alloyed candlesticks, crowns, bowls, and batons. It made no sense—definitely not economic sense—but it was very Chalcolithic.

Thousands of years after humans heeded the call to build the monumental tower in Jericho, and after centuries of permanent settlement and perfectly domesticated agriculture in most parts of the world, humanity jumped on the fast track to a new social order. This one had professional specialization, internal hierarchies, and before long also rulers and subjects. Some mined copper by the sweat of their brow; others led the convoys of donkeys in the desert; and others formed metalworking guilds, and only they knew what to do with metal ore and how. They had secret knowledge, and their social status reflected this fact. "As far as how ancient societies viewed things," says Ben-Yosef, "the ability to transform stone into another material required a connection with the gods." The ironsmiths in contemporary tribal societies in Africa are considered priests, and it is quite possible that Chalcolithic smiths had the same status. And if not exactly priests, then something close to the priesthood.

All this required the valuable material, copper ore, to be brought as close as possible to places of settlement. Stratified societies in the making could probably not afford to try to control events far away. It was important for the sources of authority and knowledge not to push their luck, but to flaunt their skills and abilities to their own neighbors in their communities.

Timothy Earle is an economic anthropologist from Northwestern University. His archeological research on the growth and existence of unequal, class-based societies has been highly praised. Earle investigated how ancient rulers amassed power and established their status in different places around the world: in Denmark, starting around 2300 BCE; in the Andes in Peru, starting in the fifth century CE; and in Hawaii, starting with the first human settlement there in the eighth century CE. In all three chronologically and geographically distinct places, the regional tribal kingdoms were created thanks to their control of production and distribution.

In Hawaii, and to some extent in the Andes, the basis of the economy changed as a result of the construction of sophisticated irrigation channels and the boosting of agricultural output. The people who spearheaded and funded the construction of irrigation networks leveraged them to amass capital and power. These savvy stakeholders used mercenaries to deprive others of free access to these networks and took over most of the land. With the irrigation system and most of the land under their ownership, it was only a simple step to seize a figurative or literal crown. In Denmark, however, the transition from the late Neolithic and the emergence of agriculture to the Bronze Age involved a boost in reciprocal trade with neighboring territories. Agricultural surpluses were a means of buying imported metals as the basis for wealth accumulation. This financial capital allowed select individuals to pursue their economic and governance objectives. Not by chance, this was also the situation in the southern Levant in the Chalcolithic period.

In his book *How Chiefs Come to Power*, Earle explains that "economic power is based on the ability to restrict access to key productive resources or consumptive goods." Elites do not need to personally control resources (such as copper or gold); it is enough to have exclusive access to the experts in the art of production, such as ironsmiths. This is a simple, even innocuous, form of control—but it is terrifyingly effective.

Earle's research relates to what archeologists call chiefdoms: a transitional stage between clan-based social structures and minor kingdoms. Chiefdoms marked the beginning of hierarchies inside groups, when people accepted the authority of one particular member as a kind of leader. This person became a tribal chief by dint of his talents, not because he was born into the right family. "Chiefdom," however, might not be exactly the right term to describe what happened in the southern Levant 6,000 years ago. Yorke Rowan, an archeologist from the University of Chicago who studies the Chalcolithic period, reminds us that there is quite a lot of evidence to prove that these were not egalitarian societies, but not of the sort to support the theory of chiefdoms.

None of the settlements had houses that looked bigger or more luxurious than others, and in fact they were all fairly similar. Nor were they found to contain the graves or burial caves of leaders; on the contrary, there were only mass, collective graves. Rowan may be right, and we can assume that bona fide chiefs were not quite sitting on thrones and doling out commands just yet. But there is no doubt that at the end of the fourth millennium BCE, the Levant was full of more than enough people who were already hungering for such a throne.

In the meantime, and in parallel, the Levant experienced an intense spurt of agricultural output, not just of grains and legumes, but also of different kinds of fruit trees and especially olive groves. Chalcolithic farmers took their basic produce a few steps forward. Nearly every paper on the Chalcolithic period recalls the "Secondary Products Revolution." They made looms to spin wool and churns to produce cheese. They invented things and honed their techniques for working with stone, ceramics, and ivory. They engaged in commerce across vast distances. Raw materials, goods, and finished products made their way from south to north and vice versa. People amassed possessions and power.

This was a relatively brief period of a few hundred years, packed full of activity and brimming with changes and growing pains. Dental findings point to a dramatic rise in tooth decay, a result of the growing consumption of sugar. Domesticated agriculture—with its figs, dates, and grapes, all sweeter than ever—was beginning to claim a heavy price from the people of this era.

***

In the early 1960s, the young State of Israel launched a sweeping archeological study of the caves of the southern Judean Desert. It was run like a military operation by the second chief-of-staff of the Israel Defense Forces, the archeologist Yigael Yadin, in collaboration with academic research institutes, volunteers from across the country, and logistical support from the Israeli Air Force. The discovery of the Dead Sea Scrolls in these desert caves a few years earlier, the fear of Bedouin antiquities robbers, and mostly the desire to confirm the truth of the legend of Bar Kokhba and his warriors, who hid in these caves during their revolt against the Roman Empire, spurred the authorities and researchers to embark on a complex operation. Four separate delegations conducted parallel excavations, gritted their teeth on winding ascents, and shimmied down wobbly rope ladders to the entrances of the caves in the wadis between the ancient fortress of Masada and the oasis of Ein Gedi.

Pessah Bar-Adon, who was made of similar stuff to Beno Rothenberg, received responsibility for Sector C, at the seasonal stream of Wadi Mishmar. Nicknamed "Aziz Effendi," Bar-Adon was easily mistaken for a desert Bedouin, although in his youth in Poland he had been a yeshiva (a type of traditional Jewish educational institute) student. During the second excavation season, after unearthing numerous fascinating findings from the second-century Jewish revolt against the Romans, Bar-Adon decided to dig into deeper and earlier periods in one of the caves. "My heart flickered with a spark of hope, that we might find the answer to the mystery of why people in the Chalcolithic period desired the caves of the Judean Desert as a place of settlement," wrote Bar-Adon. All along the towering cliff and in the caves of the desert canyons, the team found plenty of hints of human activity during this richly innovative period. And Bar-Adon's curiosity was certainly understandable, despite having no connection to Bar Kokhba and his revolt thousands of years later.

The "spark" in Bar-Adon's heart flickered just as the volunteers in the excavations were meant to switch over. Owing to logistical difficulties, many of the volunteers who were supposed to arrive failed to show up. Their predecessors decided to stay and discover by themselves whether anything else was hiding in the bowels of the caves. At dawn, they abseiled down the cliff to the cave opening. "At 2 p.m., we came across the biggest surprise," Bar-Adon wrote in his diary, and as a man with a flair for drama, that was how he ended the paragraph.

Indeed, the rest was dramatic. A student by the name of Ruth Pecherski, together with a soldier called Freddy Halperin, came across a narrow niche blocked by a sloped stone. For a whole hour, struggling to breathe because of the clouds of dust in the cave, they groped around inside until suddenly they touched something metallic. They pulled it out of the niche, passed it back, and shouted out with palpable excitement, "There's more!"

There was *a lot* more. More and more and more stunningly beautiful metal tools. Round and polished mace heads; crowns adorned with intricate horns; hollow copper cylinders topped with hooks or the heads of horned animals; a copper scepter topped with a trio of rams; a horn-shaped object with a winged bird at its tip; a series of fawns standing at the center of a metallic crescent; twisting copper jugs; chisels; axe heads; more mace heads and even more mace heads. All in all, the "Cave of the Treasure" was found to contain 429 objects, most of which were made with the sophisticated technique of lost-wax casting. They were wrapped in a fraying straw mat, along with several ivory objects, all created slightly over 6,000 years ago.

A selection from this rare treasure trove is on display at the Israel Museum, but the exhibition, unfortunately, is slightly disappointing. It is unimaginative and makes too little use of the drama around the discovery and its importance. If nobody told you, you could easily continue ambling through the (too many) exhibition halls and miss the story. The small screen onto which rare archival footage of the expedition at Wadi Mishmar is projected only exacerbates the sense of a missed opportunity. The material exists, the drama is well documented, but someone forgot to update it to the visual language of the new millennium.

Thankfully for us, on our way to the official exhibition, we stopped off at the Israel Museum's storage facilities, where we were welcomed by Nurith Goshen, the new curator of the Chalcolithic period. Her enthusiasm about the treasures hidden in the museum's basements was contagious. There is a box with tiny beads from a desert cave adjacent to the Cave of Treasure; and a purse made thousands of years ago from these beads; and an ancient necklace that you can hold in your hand and even try on; and suddenly she says, "Just a sec, you've got to see what's in this drawer." She was absolutely right, because in the drawer is a metal mace head sawn in half, and now you can see how the technique of lost-wax casting was performed. You can see how complicated it was, how many stages it took, and how accurately the artisans had to control the work: the preparation of the model, its attachment to the casing, the smelting of copper ore, the creation of a suitable alloy, the melting of the wax, and the series of consistent and coordinated actions at the end of which they pulled out a copper crown or a twisted candlestick, like a rabbit out of a hat. "For anyone who wasn't in on the secret," says Goshen, "this definitely looked like magic."

Not only was the production magical, but the treasure itself—a whole set of copper items from the Cave of Treasure— remains an unsolved mystery. What was such a trove doing in an inaccessible desert cave? Who put it there? For what purpose? Did it belong to a single, especially rich individual, a merchant on the move who had to hide his property? Or was this the property of a group of people who lived in this and adjacent caves? Did they deliberately hide the treasure or did they simply place it there? And why *there*?

The standard theory, which is also presented to visitors at the Israel Museum, links the treasure to a Chalcolithic temple discovered around Ein Gedi, some 10km (6mi) north of Wadi Mishmar. The explanation is that the temple was abandoned in a hurry, endangering its treasures, which were taken and hidden in the safest and most inaccessible spot around. This is certainly a plausible theory and would explain why so many copper objects were discovered there, but there is no evidence of a violent or destructive event at the temple that required its hasty evacuation. Another conventional explanation is that this was the hidden warehouse of a local merchant or a group of merchants. From this spot they ran their business, commissioning and dispatching high-quality utensils around the region for profit. Others have hypothesized that this was a deliberate stash of ritual objects that were considered defective and decommissioned. This is also a possibility, as plausible as the others.

In a follow-up Zoom conversation from his home in Chicago, Yorke Rowan is keen to remind us and his fellow researchers that metal ornaments were not the only things discovered in the cave. Among the discoveries were five Chalcolithic human remains, and it would be a mistake to overlook them—and the cooking, food storage, and wool-spinning implements discovered in one of the inner caverns. People lived there and were buried there, Rowan explains—a fact that sits ill at ease with the above theories.

The boldest, if not the wildest, theory of all about the treasure was proposed by Nissim Amzallag, of Ben Gurion University. Amzallag argues that the copper items were a visual code, the start of an early written language used by metalsmiths—marks based on the rebus principle, a puzzle device familiar from some crosswords and cryptic letters. In this device, the meaning of the symbols lies not in the literal translation of illustrations but in what they express phonetically or in the ideas they convey. Amzallag insists that he has identified at least twenty cryptic clues in the treasure trove from Nahal Mishmar. In his theory, these clues were used in an internal language to describe ancient metallurgical concepts.

Unsurprisingly, the reactions to this theory were furious and extreme, even for the typically critical field of academia. To Amzallag's credit, we must say that underpinning this theory— and long before the matter of visual codes—is a recognition that creating metal was inventing a new material. There was something divine about it, at least for people from a slightly earlier period from us. Hence the immense importance of the metalsmiths, the people who possessed the secret of the creation and control of copper.

The mystery of the treasure in the Nahal Mishmar Cave remains unresolved. And maybe that's a good thing. Mysteries are always more intriguing than clear conclusions. This is definitely something that the current curator of the Chalcolithic exhibitions at the Israel Museum would be wise to take into account when deciding to refresh this somewhat underwhelming exhibition.

***

The story of Chalcolithic treasures does not end here. A short hop from the exhibits of copper objects from the Judean Desert stand miniature ossuaries looking like bemused soldiers in formation from the Peki'in Cave, which was discovered in 1995. Each ossuary has a face on its front, and each face has a prominent nose and a funny twist. They look either wonky, bloated, or open-mouthed, or have comically large eyes. "These were probably people with a sense of humor," says Goshen, the curator. A five-year-old girl who has been staring at the ossuaries for a few minutes says confidently that she thinks they were once microwave ovens. That might have something to it.

Like many archeological findings, including some presented in this book, the Peki'in Cave in northern Israel was also discovered thanks to a tractor or bulldozer that nearly fell into an ancient pit. Dina Shalem, a junior archeologist at the time, received a phone call one Saturday afternoon from a flustered colleague who told her that a Chalcolithic burial cave had been discovered near a Druze village in the Upper Galilee. Shalem was sure that he was pulling her leg because she thought she knew for certain that there were no Chalcolithic burial caves in northern Israel. But certainty is a concept that should be taken with a pinch of salt in prehistoric research, and by the next morning the certainty was erased and replaced with utter astonishment.

Years later, we sat with Shalem at the Israel Antiquities Authority office in the Old City of Acre and heard how extraordinary this all was: "You climb down the ladder to a depth of only around 4m (13ft), and you reach the set of a horror movie. A dramatic scene of dozens of vases, smashed ossuaries, hundreds of skeletons scattered in such a way that your feet can't touch the ground without stepping on someone, and above all this are stalagmites and stalactites and I'd rather not tell you how they fit between the bones and the skulls. It was a once-in-a-lifetime kind of sight."

The first question that Shalem and her colleagues asked themselves that day at the foot of the ladder was: *how do we move on from here?* "How" in the most literal sense. How could they take a step forward without stepping on an urn, ossuary or, God forbid, someone who had been lying there for 6,000 years? Instead of digging for the remains, they picked them off the floor with superhuman caution and patience. One of the most striking features of this mesmerizing mess in the karstic cave was the abundant evidence of "secondary burial." In simple terms, that's the process in which dead people are temporarily buried somewhere, removed after their flesh decomposes, and their bones are stored in ornamental receptacles (ossuaries, or "microwave ovens," as the little girl in the museum put it) before being given a dignified second burial, this time for good.

"These people did something that I can't quite wrap my head around, and I'm not alone," says Shalem: they disconnected the skulls of their dear, deceased relatives and stored them separately from the rest of the bones. This practice was not invented in the Chalcolithic period. Back in Neolithic Jericho, people practiced secondary burial, with skulls decorated with seashells and beads in their eye sockets. But in the Chalcolithic period, this became almost *de rigueur*. "These guys chose to invest their precious time and skills in dealing with the dead," explains Shalem. "There must have been a reason that goes beyond any particular urn. Something happened there, there was a social vibe of leaving bodies where they were, gathering the bones, and putting them in a container called an ossuary. This was a dramatic change in burial customs, and there must have been a reason for it."

The reason, in Shalem's assessment, has to do with social changes during this period. This was a process that received expression in cultural and artistic representations all over the land, north and south, in the treasures of Wadi Mishmar and in the Peki'in Cave. "There was a leadership that led to the creation of transitional rituals. Secondary burial has a public dimension—this was a communal event, a means of social consolidation."

In our conversation, as in many of his publications, Yorke Rowan emphasizes the singular and profound significance of the subterranean world for the people of the Chalcolithic period.

"They were the first miners," he notes, "they dug deep into the ground in order to reach their metals and they used natural caves much more extensively than in the past." Secondary burial, he believes, represented an advanced stage of transitional rituals between worlds, between life and death.

Shalem is inclined to agree on this point with the scholar from Chicago, and she too believes that the Peki'in Cave was not just a subterranean chamber that happened to be available and suitable for burying the dead. Caves were apparently never just useful underground spaces—not for the Cro-Magnons in the Dordogne Valley, nor for the people who accompanied the tortoise shaman on her final journey to the Hilazon Cave, and definitely not for the Chalcolithic-era humans in the Upper Galilee. For them, as Shalem puts it in her typically blunt and jovial style, "this whole business about the cave was much more than just leaving the bones there and going."

The dozens of skeletons and skulls unearthed in Peki'in, a rare concentration by any global metric, formed the basis of an extended genetic study by Harvard University and Tel Aviv University's medical school. The study concluded that the people buried in Peki'in around 6,000 years ago represented a fusion of native Levantines with immigrants from Persia and central Anatolia. Diverse people from far-flung areas had mixed, coexisted, and interbred, and most of them, it seems, had blue eyes. It is quite possible that they were the distant ancestors of the masses of visitors—Jews, Arabs, Druze, and Circassians—who flood the alleyways of the Old City of Acre during our conversation with Shalem, looking for a nice eatery or recommended hummus joint.

Shalem, one of the authors of this genetic study, was unfazed by its ethnic discoveries. Her father was born in Djerba in Tunisia, her mother is Swedish, and she has a Chilean brother-in-law and a biracial niece. The ethnic fusion of the blue-eyed Chalcolithic humans is no competition for her own family. Migration is a natural part of human history: people have always roamed the earth, fleeing disaster, searching for possibilities, escaping problems for fresher pastures. From subjugation to liberty, from obedience to independent trade and enterprise. At the end of the next chapter, prehistory will be poised to turn into history—and there are still some things that will never, ever change.

Beno Rothenbeg (second from the left) with his camera in 1956

CHAPTER 10

LIKE THE CIRCLES OF YOUR MIND

c.5,700 years ago

**From the stone circles in the Golan Heights
to Stonehenge in southern England**

**Who built the mysterious "wildcat" heap of stones?
Why do people visit it and similar sites around the world?
How can you get a bird's eye view without wings?
And why is it worth delving into the depths of the
human soul, even when discussing prehistory?**

It's the end of the day. A gentle westerly breeze breathes life into the fields of yellowing stubble in the Golan Heights, and the reservoirs burst their banks after a bountiful winter, flooding the roads and paths. A young man, at the prime of his life, carries a heavy backpack and waits for his girlfriend to find a way to skip over the puddles so that they can continue to their destination. Others can be seen hiking to the same point, one lugging a guitar, another retrieving a flute from a colorful fabric rucksack. Around the same time, far away from here, in southern England, a young couple wearing fashionable Uniqlo jackets hold hands and march up Silbury Hill on their way to to the Avebury stone circles. A young woman squeezes between two hulks of carved stone at nearby Stonehenge, a blanket draped over her shoulders, her eyes closed. Further west, an infant peeks over the baby carrier on his father's back on the way to Newgrange in Ireland.

These people, and many others, have converged on these sites at the same moment, on the same occasion, for the same reason: to watch the sunrise on the longest day of the year. It's just as uplifting, enchanting, and mysterious a moment in the twenty-first century as it was thousands of years ago—at Avebury, Stonehenge, Newgrange—and here, at Rujm el-Hiri in the southern Golan Heights.

In the middle of the fields, with the herds of Charolais cattle that stare at passers-by with baffled expressions as if trying to understand whether they've lost something, the piles of stones in the distance look like the many heaps of rocks scattered across this basalt plateau overlooking the Sea of Galilee. Just more piles of stones. Even as you approach, unless someone draws your attention to them, you might just walk past them and miss this extraordinary spectacle. It takes a different, higher perspective—a bird's eye view—to realize that this is something else altogether, something monumental: five enormous concentric stone circles, the largest of which has a circumference of nearly half a kilometer (0.3mi). They are connected to each other with a series of internal walls, which lend the construction the appearance of a maze. In the middle of the stone circles is a raised stone tumulus, or archeological monument. This wonderful architectural surprise consists of tens of thousands of basalt rocks meticulously balanced on top of each other.

Rujm el-Hiri was discovered in an archeological survey conducted in the Golan Heights immediately after the 1967 Six-Day War. Yitzhaki Gal, an amateur archeologist, spotted something strange and intriguing in some aerial photographs: piles of stones that seemed to have been arranged in concentric circles. He was supposed to focus on archeological remains from the period of the Great Revolt against the Romans in the first century, but he decided to devote a whole day to exploring these stone circles up close. They were in the middle of nowhere, far away from any settlement or road, and it took him quite some time to hike there. Even today, the site is still hard to reach, and maybe that's part of the secret of its charm and helps to explain why it attracts so few visitors. In any case, when Yitzhaki Gal arrived and stood on the raised mound, he understood at once, even without the necessary perspective, that he was surrounded by something unique and immaculately planned. It was definitely ancient, but *how* ancient was still unclear. It was even less clear what purpose it was supposed to serve and who had built such a strange complex in the middle of nowhere.

The local Druze villagers called the site *Rujm el-Hiri*: the stone heap of the wildcat. Maybe because if you look at it head-on, the mound and basalt circles might look like a cat wrapped in its own tail. Yehudah Ziv, an accomplished Israeli geographer and a member of Israel's Government Naming Committee, proposed the Hebrew name *Gilgal Rephaim*, after the giant Rephaites of the Bible. It's definitely a catchy name, and even without the biblical allusion, it has a ring that suits the architecture and character of the site.

Monumental stone structures, and especially stone circles, are the hallmark of cultures that developed into chiefdoms at the time when those who abandoned hunting and gathering still practiced traditions from their past and were willing to obey tribal chiefs. These were the world's first socially stratified societies, where specialization existed alongside a desire to maintain unity or at least a sense of group belonging. Huge construction works that stuck out in the landscape were a proven way for societies to express this desire, as well as to achieve perfect union with the heavens, with the rising and setting of the sun, to blend into their physical surroundings and become one with it. This began thousands of years ago with the Neolithic tower at Jericho and then spread all around the globe.

The huge stone circle at Stonehenge is the most famous example. The stones, in their current form, were placed there over 4,000 years ago on top of what was a ritual site thousands of years before that. Weighing dozens of tons apiece, they were transported from miles away and arranged into exact circles, the openings lined up with sunrise and sunset on the longest and shortest days of the year (the summer and winter solstices). At Newgrange in Ireland, an enormous stone circle was erected 5,000 years ago, with a corridor of giant stone tablets in the middle, leading to an inner sanctum, probably a burial chamber. At the entrance is a narrow window, through which the sun's rays shine during sunrise on the winter solstice, illuminating the passageway and the inner chamber. There are many other similar structures around the world, mostly attributable to periods that witnessed the emergence of new governmental and social structures. They were more centralized, more authoritarian, and had growing numbers of members.

The stones at Rujm el-Hiri are not as large as those at Stonehenge and Newgrange, but as a complex with enormous architecture, the site is far more sophisticated. The first exploratory mission that tried to decipher its secrets came from Harvard University. Heading the American delegation was Yonatan Mizrahi, a young and ambitious Israeli doctoral student, who managed to bring on board not only Harvard's prestigious Archeology Department but also Anthony Aveni, an anthropologist and astronomer who had published over thirty books and effectively invented a brand-new scientific discipline: archeoastronomy. Just as rivers, mountains, elephants, mammoths, and rock shelters played a central role in the lives of prehistoric humans, so too did the sun, moon, and stars. It's impossible to understand the past without this cosmic context, which still plays a bigger role in our modern lives than other parts of the natural world. That's why this chapter began as it did, with a modern-day pilgrimage to an ancient holy site to experience the magic of sunrise.

Aveni and Mizrahi presented detailed evidence of the astronomical significance of Rujm el-Hiri. This enormous complex was built to match up with the solar system and in particular with sunrise on the longest day of the year, when the sun rises almost exactly through the northeastern opening. These stone circles are also aligned with the physical landscape, and their openings point to the surrounding mountains:

Mount Hermon on one side and Mount Tabor on the other. As you stand on the basalt rocks waiting for the sun to disperse the morning fog, the snowy peaks of Mount Hermon make a mighty impression. Seeing Mount Tabor, in the distant west, takes some imagination or at least good binoculars.

Thirty years after he led the excavations at Rujm el-Hiri, we meet Mizrahi at his rural home and find him up to his neck in academic subjects such as machine learning and personality prediction models. These are his current fields of inquiry, miles away from archeological ruins and celestial objects. Nevertheless, as with any first love, just mentioning Rujm el-Hiri is enough to reawaken old feelings, and our conversation speeds toward long-forgotten sights and exciting memories of what must have been an unusual dig at an enigmatic site.

Mizrahi's eureka moment at Rujm el-Hiri, his big discovery, came when his team ran some magnetic tests in search of empty spaces beneath the heaps of stones. This required innovative technology, and few people had access to this equipment, not to mention the knowledge demanded to use it in scientific fieldwork. Harvard, being Harvard, had the most advanced gear available, and Mizrahi decided to play around with it and see what it could do. To his astonishment, the magnetic resonance machinery picked up on a large cavern underneath the pile of stones in the middle of the circles: the elevated mound where dozens of people trod when we visited the site just before sunset. This was not a pile of basalt rocks, Mizrahi understood, but a megalithic structure in its own right: an inner chamber surrounded by huge stones around and above.

The strenuous (and admittedly somewhat destructive) excavations led the archeologists to the roof of an ancient structure, covered in tablets believed to weigh over five tons each. An optical fiber was wiggled through a crack between the tablets and sent back images that showed that the chamber contained a room built of stone. The crack was then widened enough to allow a volunteer to slink through it into the mysterious room. The Druze laborers were horrified by what might be buried there, and Mizrahi's ex-army friends were too broad-shouldered to squeeze through. The job fell to a lanky young man by the name of Matti Zohar, who had walked all the way from Germany to participate in the excavation and was willing to sign up for anything. But after all these preparations— and amid palpable tension—came disappointment. Inside, they found a round room, 2m (6.5ft) in diameter and 1.5m (5ft) high, entered through a passageway just a few metres long, but the room and the passageway were empty. There was absolutely nothing inside.

Like the tower at Jericho, which was effectively a stone container for the staircase inside, so too did this pile of stones in the middle of Rujm el-Hiri envelop the room and the passageway. This kind of architecture is familiar from many stone circles around Europe: a corridor, an inner chamber, and a stone elevation. Human remains were discovered in only a few of these chambers, but everyone agreed that they were originally built as impressive burial structures. Thanks to the passageways, they came to be known as "passage graves."

As Timothy Earle writes in his book *How Chiefs Come to Power*, megalithic burial structures had great symbolic and practical significance. They were built to protrude into the horizon and serve as a rock-solid confirmation of ownership over the surrounding agricultural lands. It took thousands of hours of manpower to build them, to make it obvious to anyone glancing at them who was in charge and what status was held by the people buried there and their descendants. Despite certain similarities between the megalithic structures that Earle discusses and the one in the Golan Heights, it's doubtful whether we can accept his theory, and especially its consequentialist logic, in full. Rujm el-Hiri is much more sophisticated, and it blends into the landscape rather than competes with it. This was not a muscular assertion of ownership. It was something much more spiritual.

***

The metal detector inserted into the passage grave at Rujm el-Hiri managed to reveal, under a layer of earth, a few gold earrings and metal instruments from the Late Bronze Age. That's several thousand years after the period when the site was built, and deep into the history of kings, cities, and other troubles. The Harvard expedition focused more on astronomy than chronology, and its members could live with attributing the stone circles to the Early Bronze Age and the additional burial structure to the Late Bronze Age: 3,300 and 1,500 BCE respectively.

But this chronological sequence made no sense to at least one researcher, Michael Freikman, who also wrote his doctoral thesis on this mysterious site. Freikman is an expert in the archeology of landscapes, in how prehistoric humans arranged and experienced the spaces they lived in. And what vexed him at Rujm el-Hiri was the landscape, or rather, what was missing from the landscape—any nearby Bronze Age settlements. Without them, it was a complete mystery who built these stone circles and why.

However, Rujm el-Hiri *is* encircled on all sides by Chalcolithic settlement sites. The Golan Heights are littered with dolmens—huge table-like stone structures that served as tombs—attached to the walls of Chalcolithic houses. What could be more logical than to assume that Rujm el-Hiri was also a Chalcolithic site? That these stone circles, for all their sophistication, size, and planning, were a majestic expression of the same social, spiritual, and economic needs that humanity has known for millennia?

We meet Freikman between the stone circles, which have become a part of his life, just as he—it seems—has become a part of them. He walks around Rujm el-Hiri like it's his backyard: he's familiar with nearly every hunk of rock, and he is used to sleeping on the black tuff soil. "The landscape is the most important factor, its visibility is the key," Freikman says as the first rays of sunlight rise from the east on the morning of the longest day of the year, to the sound of trumpets and cheering from those who have spent the night here. "This site," he explains, "is a statement of a society's ideology. Like the Arc de Triomphe on the Champs-Elysées or the menorah outside the Knesset building in Jerusalem. These are prominent landmarks that interact with their surroundings. Rujm el-Hiri doesn't fit the urban periods, which came later. This wasn't a place for worshipping a leader. This was a place to communicate with other worlds. Don't take my word for it. That's what the Rujm itself says."

Freikman's feet are planted firmly on the ground, and New Age spirituality doesn't really do it for him. He bases his arguments on similar examples from the same period—on established archeological knowledge about pre-urban rites. This is a form of worship familiar to us from Chapter 7, one connected to the world of the dead, which brings the underworld and the heavens into communion through a shaman. It's possible that this megalithic structure served the work of a local Chalcolithic shaman. In terms of the stone circles, the conclusions of this Hebrew University academic are not much different from those of the Harvard delegation: they marked the *axis mundi*, the axis of the Earth between the celestial poles, and were built with reference to the stars and the angle of sunrise on the longest day of the year. Freikman sees the mound of stones in the middle and the space beneath it as a replica mound and cave: an artificial reconstruction of two hugely important features of the world of prehistoric humans—a mountain, on the way to higher worlds, and a cave, as the gate to the underworld. Rujm el-Hiri, with its mountain, cave, and stone circles, is a ritual and symbolic landmark that unites these two worlds in the lives of human beings.

Freikman found the telltale clue about when this complex was built thanks to an exact dating system that tests when grains of sand were first exposed to sunlight. The discovery of a small sand trap underneath the complex made it possible to say with certainty that its foundations were built no later than 3,740 BCE. That dates it to the late Chalcolithic, a period defined by a mysterious crisis that led to the collapse of civilizations. The Bronze Age in the Levant would only arrive a few centuries later; it would build, to a large extent, on the ruins of this unexplained crisis.

All of this—the relationships between the site and celestial elements and new results from precise dating—should have finally cracked the mystery of the wildcat stones. But then, none other than Carl Gustav Jung entered the picture. Or rather, his theory did.

***

Carl Jung, a student of Sigmund Freud, turned his back on his teacher's theories because of a dream. His dream began in an unfamiliar two-story house. Jung walked down to the ground floor, meandered between the antique medieval furniture and reached a door leading to the basement. He followed the stairs down, past walls last plastered in antiquity, and from there continued even deeper, into a cave hewn into the rock. This, he wrote in his autobiography *Memories, Dreams, Reflections*, was a "prehistoric cave": "In the dust were scattered bones and broken pottery, like remains of a primitive culture. I discovered two human skulls, obviously very old and half disintegrated. Then I awoke."

Jung coined a new term, which became fundamental to his theory: the "collective subconscious." This is what the prehistoric cave represents: the unconscious part of the mind shared by all humanity, rooted in universal experiences and events from the past, in archetypes preserved in our memory, crossing cultures and time periods. This was the beginning of a new way of understanding the recesses of the human psyche.

In the early twentieth century, Jung investigated circular models and structures called *mandalas*, used by various cultures in the Far East. He saw that whenever there was a threat to the unity of a people or its way of life, they got together to build mandalas. These buildings symbolized their hopes and efforts to restore harmony and order. Mandalas appeared in the dreams of Jung's patients and his colleagues. They cropped up especially when patients were suffering from stress and confusion and experienced chaotic situations. Jung explained that this was an archetypal model that aids recovery. The process of creating mandalas allows individuals and groups in crisis to find peace of mind.

Many years after Jung devised these insights, the Israeli psychoanalyst Micha Ankori joined his daughter for a hike around the Golan Heights. He remembers the moment he saw Rujm el-Hiri and realized that it was not just any old megalithic structure, but another of Jung's mandalas. "I've got a feeling I know what's going on," he told his daughter and explained what he had learned from the Swiss psychologist and what all this had to do with what looked like a random pile of rocks.

Ankori has an unconventional life story. He was a mathematician and a physicist before becoming a clinical psychologist. He is a founding member of the Israel Institute for Jungian Psychology, a pioneering educator, and one of the leading scholars of the psychological dimensions of Kabbalah and the Hasidic movement. The fact he makes an appearance here, in a story about a prehistoric journey, is a welcome and meaningful addition. After all, there is nothing more fascinating than the human psyche. It is what lurks deep with us, *Homo sapiens* or Neanderthals or Denisovans, or for that matter, *Homo erectus*. It is in the humans of today, yesterday, the day before yesterday, and tomorrow, Here, and in the heart of Africa, and far away in Arctic wastelands. It's in what happened during the stormy Chalcolithic or Early Bronze Age, and whatever is coming up soon. All of them—and all of us—are alike.

"What attracts me is human nature," Ankori tells us in a conversation as we near the end of writing our book. "Humans are the products of culture, but the further back you go, there are fewer and fewer layers of culture and more human nature. And that's what Jung does. All our knowledge about the past— like archeology or anthropology—reveals a human unity. That humans are one big family. Genetic research shows the same thing. We're all the children of the same mother from Africa. Deep in the human psyche there's unity, and one of its archetypal models is the mandala." And if the mandala is an archetypal model, you can understand why stone circles keep cropping up in different places, cultures, and times. This isn't knowledge or technology moved from place to place; it's something deeper in the depths of the human soul.

But we are still left wondering why this mandala can only be seen from a bird's eye view. Ankori's answer is clear-cut: "You can't see gravity either, but it exists. You don't have to see the source of order to know that it exists. I can take part in building it, and even if I won't be able to see anything, it's still a part of me."

But maybe they *did* see these stone circles, actually *see* them, from above? Just as it's possible that from a great height, Peru's famous Nazca Lines were also visible. Not with a drone, nor even with a hot air balloon, but in an altered state of mind: a trance induced by a prehistoric shaman. The Cro-Magnons in the Dordogne Valley touched the animals they hunted on the walls of caves deep underground; Dandan Bolotin saw the goddess of the forests watching him in the jungles of Ecuador; and maybe Chalcolithic-era humans also wafted over Rujm el-Hiri in their dreams?

Either way, these stone circles, according to Ankori and his Jungian theories, encapsulate all the meanings attributed to them by various scholars: they formed an astronomical wheel, expressing a longing for cosmic unity, an *axis mundi* that corresponded with the mountain that loomed above it; this was a ritual site occupied by a shaman, the receptacle of generations of wisdom and knowledge, and the creator of unity between humans and their gods; and it was a structure that helped its builders and pilgrims to find psychic harmony.

Both 6,000 years ago and yesterday at sunset.

***

It's afternoon, and the sun, having cast its magical rays through the apertures of stone circles at sites around the world, has climbed to the middle of the sky; the crowds disperse as people go back to their business, to their daily lives. Tents are packed away, musical instruments are returned to their cases, and across the Golan Heights jeeps leave behind clouds of dust, disturbing the herds of cattle as they trundle along.

Our prehistoric journey has ended. If we take a few steps forward, we'll reach written history. We'll read about cities and states, about kings and dukes and armies, about crusades, world wars, and death camps. The world will be belligerent and patriarchal, and the harmony between humanity and nature will be rudely interrupted. Empires will rise and fall, human migration will accelerate, Apollo 11 will land on the moon, and Neil Armstrong will call this step small for man and large for mankind, coining the sort of successful slogan that reshapes our world. The Chalcolithic period in the Levant and the late Neolithic in Europe mark the end of an extremely long, winding, hazardous journey that we have only touched upon. A road full of achievements and more than our fair share of unavoidable mistakes. And all of it, for better or worse, was thanks to those who were here before us. From now on, it's all up to us.

Mysterious stone circles at Rujm el-Hiri

EPILOGUE OR
LONG AFTER US

The American actor and stand-up comedian Marc Maron has a televised show called *End Times Fun*, in which he says:

> I don't know what's happening, people, I don't know. But it's pretty clear the world is ending. I don't want to shock anybody. Seems to be happening though. I thought we'd get it out. I thought we'd make it under the wire. I thought I would, you know. I'm fifty-six, but I don't know, I think we might see it . . . Certainly it's been ending environmentally for a long time. And we've all kind of known it, we knew it, but I think on a deeper level, the reason we're not more upset about the world ending environmentally is I think all of us, in our hearts really know that we did everything we could. Right? I mean, we really did. I mean, think about it, we brought our own bags to the supermarket . . . Yeah, that's about it. And it just wasn't enough, it turns out. Just not enough to get us over the top with this. But I don't know, maybe this straw thing, the no-straw thing, will, you know, maybe that'll do it. Maybe that'll keep the polar bears from drowning.

As we know, the scientific data about humanity's future is extremely concerning. Recent studies show that since the 1970s, we have driven 60 per cent of all the mammal, bird, reptile, and fish species on Planet Earth to extinction. The "Sixth Extinction" is already a part of our reality, and it's our responsibility alone.

Time and again, to the point of nagging, we have tried throughout this book to highlight the deep, ongoing relationship between humans and other animals and to present the massive influence of megafauna on our lives. The disappearance of prehistoric elephants hundreds of thousands of years ago, the extinction of woolly mammoths 15,000 years ago, and the dwindling presence of other huge mammals, which might have been one of the catalysts of the Prehistoric Agricultural Revolution—these were all major junctions that led to far-reaching changes in the story of humankind: technological innovations, dietary changes, migrations to ever-further distances, and the creation of new social structures. And still, in all likelihood, at none of these prehistoric junctions was the situation as dramatic as the one we face now. If only because of the regrettable fact that the mind-bogglingly quick extermination of so many animal species is not our only problem.

Little more than 6,000 years have passed since the last chapter in our journey. It's the blink of an eye, a momentary flurry of events. If you were to compress the whole of earth's history into a single calendar year, humankind would only appear in the last few hours of December, and the past 6,000 years would be no more than a few clicks of the second hand. The Bronze Age and the Iron Age, walled cities and kingdoms, empires that rose, fell, and disappeared, gods and temples, the Byzantine Empire, the Middle Ages, the Crusades, two world wars, the moon landing, ballistic missiles, the atom bomb, the invention of the wheel, all-inclusive vacations, reality TV, and therapy appointments on Zoom—all these and so much more happened after the end of this book, once the past became simply *history*. For most of the time, life was bad. Sometimes, it was really bad. Cities and states did not bring wellbeing and prosperity for their inhabitants, but overcrowding, suffering, and disease. The invention of writing was directly linked to taxation and bigger workloads. And the transition to agriculture, as we have shown, did not necessarily improve the human diet and definitely led to the creation of stratified societies, with rulers and subjects. The *Homo erectus* who walked out of Africa nearly two million years ago and stopped for a long lakeside break in the Jordan Valley wouldn't stick around for a minute. They would probably turn around and report that human beings had gone mad.

In his wonderful book *Humankind: A Hopeful History*, the Dutch historian Rutger Bregman writes: "Our sense of history gets flipped upside down. Civilization has become synonymous with peace and wilderness with war and decline. In reality, for most of human existence, it was the other way around." In our long march from what was probably a kind of heaven on earth toward an uncertain future, we have adopted a lofty view of the world that we live in. Not only in how we see ourselves as the top of the pyramid and the purpose of all creation, but also in how we have belittled and dismissed any alternatives. We have made ourselves deaf to things that were once part of our world, and which once allowed us to live at a more reasonable, less anxious pace than now. Prehistoric humans saw woolly mammoths staring at them from the walls of caves deep underground, let their minds wander far above stone circles, knew every bush and every path in their surroundings, and were aware that next to the sheer might of nature, they were nothing. They had a much more intricate and holistic worldview than we do.

In another 2,000 or 5,000 years, assuming humanity survives till then, archeologists will dig up evidence of an extremely impressive civilization. Impressive, but also overcrowded and overshadowed by questions about its "carrying capacity": its potential to provide a healthy and stable existence for hundreds of millions of humans. Future archeologists will undoubtedly have something to say about the inconceivable mass of objects we have accumulated. A quick look in a kitchen drawer in the ruins of a standard twenty-first-century house would show just how full our lives are of objects, and how dependent on them we are.

Ian Hodder, an archeologist we cited only briefly in our chapter on the Neolithic Revolution, focuses in his research on the significance of the connection between human beings and their useful possessions. "The human dependence on and attachment to things we have created are directly related to the problem of global warming," writes Hodder in his book *Where Are We Heading?* He cites the example of the sickle, a tool that humans invented thousands of years ago to streamline the harvest. This tool led to the development of industrialized agriculture, which is currently responsible for 18 per cent of all greenhouse gas emissions in the world. The Chalcolithic spinning loom, a major step in the Secondary Products Revolution that we covered in Chapter 9, led us to the cotton industry, which consumes some 2,500 liters (700 gallons) of water just to create a single T-shirt. We solved problems by inventing efficient and useful objects that created new problems, and so the cycle continues.

Hodder proposes that when thinking about the future, we should consider what already happened in the past and adopt a multi-layered, archeological perspective. "We cannot keep doing what we have always done—find short-term technological solutions that lock us into long-term pathways," he writes. He also asks us to learn a thing or two from indigenous societies, which behave differently from Western cultures—such as Aboriginal Australians and their land conservation practices. By controlling forest fires in sophisticated ways, they promised themselves lives of ecological diversity and a basis for sustainable growth for millennia. The Aborigines never had to put up with the sort of terrible bushfires that make news nearly every summer in modern Australia. These fires are the direct result of the complete opposite of the approach of indigenous peoples: the overexploitation of land and the neglect of oversight in favor of maximizing output and satisfying immediate gains.

***

Not everything is dark and gloomy, of course, not now and not in the foreseeable future. If there is one thing that we can learn from the behavior of humankind in these ten chapters, it is that it knows how to get on in life. Intellectual flexibility, creativity, and collaboration lifted us out of terrible crises and opened fresh opportunities for us. We can go back to the Qesem Cave 400,000 years ago and marvel at how humanity overcame the catastrophe that left them without the bulk of their livelihoods. They didn't sit around, whining about their bitter fate and waiting for the elephants to return. They reinvented themselves and carried on.

One of the most fascinating chapters in Bregman's book is about the mystery of the giant statues on Easter Island in the Pacific Ocean. Ever since the arrival of the first Europeans, back in the early eighteenth century, people have tried to understand why these sculptures were built. How were they transported there from distant quarries? Why are there no trees on the islands? And most importantly, what happened to the local population, only a few dozen of whom survived? Prejudice and sloppy scholarship led to the myth that human hostility and aggression explain this mystery. It was claimed that two rival tribes had competed to build giant statues; the struggle and the constant need to transport these statues led to intense deforestation; and when no trees remained, violence escalated, the islanders attacked each other, and things got so bad that they cannibalized each other.

Bregman, a passionate believer in human nature, breaks down the muddle-headed myths, tracks down the source of these prejudices, and points to a completely different narrative about what happened to the Easter Islanders. They lived in perfect harmony, and that was how they built and transported their monumental sculptures together. They neither eradicated their island's trees nor fought each other, and they certainly didn't eat each other. Instead, a series of ecological catastrophes (such as the appearance of a new species of rat, which caused irredeemable damage to trees) forced them to find new and original livelihoods. They exploited deforested areas to grow crops, cultivated the exposed soil, and collaborated in the struggle against natural disasters. This is not a story of doom and gloom, but an optimistic tale about human ingenuity and the ability to escape crises . . . until the slavers came and finally annihilated those who remained.

"Too many environmental activists underestimate the resilience of humankind," writes Bregman, concerned that cynical despair about our situation will become a self-fulfilling prophecy. We don't have an action plan; that's not our job, and it's definitely not our expertise. But we think that our prehistoric journey—even when it veered far from what we consider paradise—should provide a measure of hope about our ability to save ourselves from a gloomy future.

It might have been a mistake on our part to climb down from trees several million years ago. Perhaps we would have been better off staying in Africa or keeping our heads down and knapping hand axes, which worked well enough for long enough. It's definitely a shame we didn't make a bit more of an effort to keep the Neanderthals around, and maybe another species or two of humans. Obviously, we would have thought twice if someone had warned us what would happen after we started domesticating plants and animals, and it's doubtful we'd have heeded the call 10,000 years ago to build a tower in Jericho or to start turning rocks into metals a few thousand years after that. But this is the path we have chosen, and it has taken us to some wild and fascinating places. There is no point trying to settle old scores with the past or whining about the future.

There were people here before us, and we should do the best we can to make sure that there will also be people here after us.

SOURCES

The following is a list of sources for the direct quotes in the text.

Chapter 1

Ehrenreich, B. "Humans were not centre stage". *Guardian.* 12 December 2019.

Bar-Yosef, O., & Belfer-Cohen, A. 2001. "From Africa to Eurasia: early dispersals". *Quaternary International* 75(1), 19–28.

Rak, Y. 2018. "The fossil evidence for human evolution". Rector lecture series, Tel-Aviv University. TAUVOD. (in Hebrew).

Bryson, B. 2003. *A Short History of Nearly Everything.* Broadway Books.

Chapter 2

Kohn, M., & Mithen, S. 1999. "Handaxes: products of sexual selection?". *Antiquity* 73, 518–526.

Cooke, L. 2017. *The Unexpected Truth About Animals.* Doubleday.

Lewis, J. 2015. "Where goods are free but knowledge costs: hunter-gatherer ritual economics in Western Central Africa". *Hunter Gatherer Research* 1(1), 1–27.

Chapter 3

Arthur, K. W. 2018. *The Lives of Stone Tools.* University of Arizona Press.

Abad, H. "A rationalist in the jungle". In: *Granta Travel* 124, 103–126.

Chapter 4

Chait, C. 2018. *No Time and the Missing Link*. Self published. (in Hebrew).

Wrangham, R. 2009. *Catching Fire: How Cooking Made Us Human*. Profile Books.

Pyne, S. J. 2019. *Fire: A Brief History*. University of Washington Press.

Chapter 5

Garrod, G., & Bate D. M. A. 1937. *The Stone Age of Mount Carmel: Excavations at the Wady Elmughara Vol. I*. Clarendon Press. Oxford.

Chapter 6

Diamond, J. 1997. *Guns, Germs, and Steel: The Fates of Human Societies*. Simon & Schuster. New York.

Harrari, Y. N. 2014. *Sapiens: A Brief History of Humankind*. Random House.

Bryson, B. *A Short History of Nearly Everything*. Broadway Books.

Miller, H. 2010. *The Colossus of Maroussi*. New Directions Publishing.

Clottes, J. 2013. "Why Did They Draw in Those Caves?". *Time and Mind* 6(1), 7–14.

Chapter 7

Stiner, M. C. 2017. "Love and death in the Stone Age: what constitutes first evidence of mortuary treatment of the human body?". *Biological Theory* 12(4), 248–261.

Naveh, D. 2020. "People of the Nayake". Podcast. The Laboratory. KAN Israeli Public Broadcasting Corp. (in Hebrew).

Kopenawa, D. 2013. *The Falling sky: Words of a Yanomami Shaman*. Harvard University Press.

Tanner, A. 2014. *Bringing Home Animals: Religious Ideology and Mode of Production of the Mistassini Cree Hunters*, 2nd edn. ISER Books. Newfoundland.

Chapter 8

Diamond, J. 1987. "The worst mistake in human history". *Discover* 8(5), 64–66.

Cauvin, J. 2000. *The Birth of the Gods and the Origins of Agriculture.* Cambridge University Press.

Hodder, I. 1990. *The Domestication of Europe: Structure and Contingency in Neolithic Societies.* Blackwell. Oxford.

Chapter 9

Rothenberg, B. 1962. *God's Wilderness: Discoveries in Sinai.* T. Nelson & Sons. New York.

Earle, T. K. 1997. *How Chiefs Come to Power: The Political Economy in Prehistory.* Stanford University Press.

Bar-Adon, P. 1980. *The Cave of Treasure. The Finds from the Caves in Nahal Mishmar.* Israel Exploration Society. Jerusalem.

Amzaleg, N. 2008. *The Copper Revolution.* Cave Publishing House. (in Hebrew).

Chapter 10

Jung, C. G. 1965. *Memories, Dreams, Reflections.* Vintage Books. New York.

EPILOGUE OR LONG AFTER US

Maron, M. 2020. *The End of the World.* Netflix

Hodder, I. 2018. *Where Are We Heading?* Yale University Press.

Berman, R. 2020. *Humankind: A Hopeful History.* Little, Brown.

FURTHER READING

General Archeology

Gamble, C. 2015. *Archaeology: The Basics*. Routledge. Abingdon.

Levy, T. E. (ed.). 1998. *The Archaeology of Society in the Holy Land*. Leicester University Press. London.

Renfrew, C., & Bahn, P. (eds.). 2014. *The Cambridge World Prehistory*. Cambridge University Press. Cambridge.

Scarre, C. (ed.). 2005. *The Human Past: World Prehistory and the Development of Human Societies*. Thames & Hudson. London.

Chapter 1

Books

Ardrey, R. 1961. *African Genesis: A Personal Investigation into the Animal Origins and Nature of Man*. Atheneum. New York.

Ardrey, R. 1977. *The Hunting Hypothesis: A Personal Conclusion Concerning the Evolutionary Nature of Man*. Fontana/ Collins. London.

Bar-Yosef, O., & Goren-Inbar, N. 1993. *The Lithic Assemblages of 'Ubeidiya: A Lower Palaeolithic Site in the Jordan Valley*. Hebrew University of Jerusalem. Jerusalem.

Dawkins, R. 1989. *The Selfish Gene*. Oxford University Press. Oxford and New York.

Fleagle, J. G., Shea, J. J., Grine, F. E., Baden, A. L., & Leakey, R. E. (eds.). 2010. *Out of Africa Volume I: The First Hominin Colonization of Eurasia*. Springer Science & Business Media. New York.

Humphrey, L., & Stringer, C. 2018. *Our Human Story: Where We Come From and How We Evolved*. Natural History Museum. London.

Lieberman, D. 2014. *The Story of the Human Body: Evolution, Health and Disease*. Penguin Vintage. London.

Roberts, A. 2018. *Evolution: The Human Story*. Dorling Kindersley. London.

Schick, K. D., & Toth, N. P. 1994. *Making Silent Stones Speak: Human Evolution and the Dawn of Technology*. Simon & Schuster. New York.

Stringer, C., & Andrews, P. 2005. *The Complete World of Human Evolution*. Thames & Hudson. London.

Tattersall, I. (1999). *Becoming Human: Evolution and Human Uniqueness*. Houghton Mifflin Harcourt. Boston (MA).

Papers

Alemseged, Z. 2014. "Early hominins". In: Renfrew, C., & Bahn, P. (eds.). *The Cambridge World Prehistory*, 47–64.

Antón, S. C., & Swisher, III, C. C. 2004. "Early dispersals of Homo from Africa". *Annual Review of Anthropology* 33, 271–296.

Bar-Yosef, O. 1994. "The Lower Paleolithic of the Near East". *Journal of World Prehistory* 8(3), 211–265.

Bar-Yosef, O., & Belmaker, M. 2011. "Early and Middle Pleistocene faunal and hominins dispersals through Southwestern Asia". *Quaternary Science Reviews* 30(11–12), 1318–1337.

Barash, A., Belmaker, M., Bastir, M., Soudack, M., O'Brien, H. D., Woodward, H., Prendergast, A., Barziali, O., & Been, E. (2022). "The earliest Pleistocene record of a large-bodied hominin from the Levant supports two out-of-Africa dispersal events". *Scientific Reports* 12(1), 1721.

Belfer-Cohen, A., & Goren-Inbar, N. 1994. "Cognition and communication in the Levantine Lower Palaeolithic". *World Archaeology* 26(2), 144–157.

Belmaker, M., Tchernov, E., Condemi, S., & Bar-Yosef, O. 2002. "New evidence for hominid presence in the Lower Pleistocene of the Southern Levant". *Journal of Human Evolution* 43(1), 43–56.

Braun, D. R. 2014. "Earliest industries of Africa". In: Renfrew, C., & Bahn, P. (eds.). *The Cambridge World Prehistory*, 65–79.

Fleagle, J. G., & Grine, F. E. 2014. "The genus Homo in Africa". In: Renfrew, C., & Bahn, P. (eds.). *The Cambridge World Prehistory*, 85–105.

Sharon, G. 2014. "The early prehistory of Western and Central Asia". In: Renfrew, C., & Bahn, P. (eds.). *The Cambridge World Prehistory*, 1357–1378.

Chapter 2

Books

Alperson-Afil, N., & Goren-Inbar, N. 2010. *The Acheulian Site of Gesher Benot Ya'aqov Volume II: Ancient Flames and Controlled Use of Fire*. Springer. New York.

Douglas-Hamilton, I., & Douglas-Hamilton, O. 1975. *Among the Elephants*. Doubleday. New York.

Gamble, C. 1999. *The Palaeolithic Societies of Europe*. Cambridge University Press. Cambridge.

Goren-Inbar, N., Alperson-Afil, N., Sharon, G., & Herzlinger, G. 2018. *The Acheulian Site of Gesher Benot Ya'aqov Volume IV: The Lithic Assemblages*. Springer Science & Business Media. New York.

Konidaris, G. E., Barkai, R., Tourloukis, V., & Harvati, K. (2021). *Human–elephant Interactions: From Past to Present*. Universität Tübingen Press. Tübingen.

Papers

Agam, A., & Barkai, R. 2018. "Elephant and mammoth hunting during the Paleolithic: a review of the relevant archaeological, ethnographic and ethno-historical records". *Quaternary* 1(1), 3.

Barkai, R. 2019. "An elephant to share: rethinking the origins of meat and fat sharing in Palaeolithic societies". In: Lavi, N., & Friesman, D. E. (eds.). *Towards a Broader View of Hunter-*

Gatherer Sharing. McDonald Institute for Archaeological Research. Cambridge, 153–167.

Barkai, R. 2020. "Lower Paleolithic bone handaxes and chopsticks: tools and symbols?". *Proceedings of the National Academy of Sciences* 117(49), 30892–30893.

Barkai, R. 2021. "The elephant in the handaxe: Lower Palaeolithic ontologies and representations". *Cambridge Archaeological Journal* 31(2), 349–361.

Ben-Dor, M., & Barkai, R. (2021). "Prey size decline as a unifying ecological selecting agent in Pleistocene human evolution". *Quaternary* 4(1), 7.

Binford, L. R. 1987. "Were there elephant hunters in Torralba?". In: Nitecki, M. H., & Nitecki, D. V. (eds.). *The Evolution of Human Hunting*. Plenum Press. New York, 47–105.

Dembitzer, J., Barkai, R., Ben-Dor, M., & Meiri, S. 2022. "Levantine overkill: 1.5 million years of hunting down the body size distribution". *Quaternary Science Reviews* 276, 107316.

Finkel, M., & Barkai, R. 2018. "The Acheulean handaxe technological persistence: a case of preferred cultural conservatism?". *Proceedings of the Prehistoric Society* 84, 1–19.

Finkel, M., & Barkai, R. 2021. "Technological persistency following faunal stability during the Pleistocene: a model for reconstructing Paleolithic adaptation strategies based on mosaic evolution". *L'Anthropologie* 125(1), 102839.

Gaudzinski-Windheuser, S., Kindler, L., MacDonald, K., & Roebroeks, W. 2023. "Hunting and processing of straight-tusked elephants 125.000 years ago: implications for Neanderthal behavior". *Science Advances* 9(5), eadd8186.

Goren-Inbar, N. 2011. "Culture and cognition in the Acheulian industry: a case study from Gesher Benot Ya'aqov". *Philosophical Transactions of the Royal Society B: Biological Sciences* 366(1567), 1038–1049.

Goren-Inbar, N., Feibel, C. S., Verosub, K. L., Melamed, Y., Kislev, M. E., Tchernov, E., & Saragusti, I. 2000. "Pleistocene milestones on the out-of-Africa corridor at Gesher Benot Ya'aqov, Israel". *Science* 289(5481), 944–947.

Goren-Inbar, N., Lister, A., Werker, E., & Chech, M. 1994. "A butchered elephant skull and associated artifacts from the Acheulian site of Gesher Benot Ya'aqov, Israel". *Paléorient* 1994, 99–112.

Guil-Guerrero, J. L., Tikhonov, A., Ramos-Bueno, R. P., Grigoriev, S., Protopopov, A., Savvinov, G., & González-Fernández, M. J. 2018. "Mammoth resources for hominins: from omega-3 fatty acids to cultural objects". *Quaternary Science* 33(4), 455–463.

Ichikawa, M. 1983. "An examination of the hunting-dependent life of the Mbuti Pygmies, Eastern Zaire". *African Study Monographs* 4, 55–76.

Kohn, M., & Mithen, S. 1999. "Handaxes: products of sexual selection?". *Antiquity* 73, 518–526.

Lewis, J. 2015. "Where goods are free but knowledge costs". *Hunter Gatherer Research* 1(1), 1–28.

Shipman, P., & Rose, J. 1983. "Evidence of butchery and hominid activities at Torralba and Ambrona: an evaluation using microscopic techniques". *Archaeological Science* 10(5), 465–474.

Villa, P., Soto, E., Santonja, M., Pérez-González, A., Mora, R., Parcerisas, J., & Sesé, C. 2005. "New data from Ambrona: closing the hunting versus scavenging debate". *Quaternary International* 126, 223–250.

Zohar, I., Alperson-Afil, N., Goren-Inbar, N., Prévost, M., Tütken, T., Sisma-Ventura, G., . . . & Najorka, J. 2022. "Evidence for the cooking of fish 780,000 years ago at Gesher Benot Ya'aqov, Israel". *Nature Ecology & Evolution* 6(12), 2016–2028.

Zutovski, K., & Barkai, R. 2016. "The use of elephant bones for making Acheulian handaxes: a fresh look at old bones". *Quaternary International* 406, 227–238.

Chapter 3
Books

Dean, C. J. 2010. *A Culture of Stone: Inka Perspectives on Rock.* Duke University Press. Durham (NC).

Hampton, O. W. 1999. *Culture of Stone: Sacred and Profane Uses of Stone among the Dani.* Texas A&M University Press. College Station (TX).

Ohel, M. Y. 1986. *The Acheulean of the Yiron Plateau, Israel* (BAR International Series). BAR Publishing. Oxford.

Ohel, M. 1991. *Prehistory of the Baram Plateau, Israel.* Department of Sociology and Anthropology, University of Haifa. Haifa.

Topping, P., & Lynott, M. 2005. *The Cultural Landscape of Prehistoric Mines.* Oxbow Books. Oxford.

Turville-Petre, F., Bate, A. J., Baynes, C., & Keith, A. 1927. *Researches in Prehistoric Galilee, 1925–1926.* Council of the British School of Archaeology in Jerusalem. London.

Papers

Barkai, R., Gopher, A., & La Porta, P. C. 2002. "Paleolithic landscape of extraction: flint surface quarries and workshops at Mt. Pua, Israel". *Antiquity* 76, 672–680.

Barkai, R., & Gopher, A. 2011. "Two flint caches from a Lower-Middle Paleolithic flint extraction and workshop complex at Mount Pua, Israel". In: *2nd International Conference of the UISPP Commission on Flint Mining in Pre and Protohistoric Times, British Archaeological Reports International Series,* 265–274.

Burton, J. 1984. "Quarrying in tribal societies". *World Archaeology* 16(2), 234–247.

Finkel, M., Gopher, A., & Barkai, R. 2016. "Extensive Paleolithic flint extraction and reduction complexes in the Nahal Dishon central basin, Upper Galilee, Israel". *World Prehistory* 29(3), 217–266.

Finkel, M., Barkai, R., Gopher, A., Tirosh, O., & Ben-Yosef, E. 2019. "The 'Flint Depot' of prehistoric northern Israel:

comprehensive geochemical analyses of flint extraction and reduction complexes and implications for provenance studies". *Geoarchaeology* 34(6), 661–683.

Foley, R. A., & Lahr, M. M. 2015. "Lithic landscapes: early human impact from stone tool production on the central Saharan environment". *PLoS One* 10(3), e0116482.

Ohel, M. Y. 1986. "Milking the stones; or an Acheulean aggregation locality on the Yiron Plateau in Upper Galilee". *Proceedings of the Prehistoric Society* 52, 247–280.

Petraglia, M., LaPorta, P., & Paddayya, K. 1999. "The first Acheulian quarry in India: stone tool manufacture, biface morphology and behaviors. *Anthropological Research* 55, 39–70.

Salas Carreño, G. 2017. "Mining and the living materiality of mountains in Andean societies". *Material Culture* 22(2), 133–150.

Chapter 4

Books

Adams, D. and Carwardine, M. 1990. *Last Chance to See*. Heinemann. Portsmouth.

Gopher A. and Tsuk T. (eds.). 1996. *The Nahal Qanah Cave: Earliest Gold in the Levant*. Tel Aviv University Institute of Archaeology Monograph Series 12. Tel Aviv.

Wrangham, R. 2009. *Catching Fire: How Cooking Made Us Human*. Basic Books. New York.

Papers

Barkai, R., & Gopher, A. 2013. "Cultural and biological transformations in the Middle Pleistocene Levant: a view from Qesem Cave, Israel". In: Akazawa, T., Nishiaki. Y., and Aoki, K. (eds.). *Dynamics of Learning in Neanderthals and Modern Humans* 1. Springer. Tokyo, 115–137.

Barkai, R., Gopher, A., Lauritzen, S. E., & Frumkin, A. 2003. "Uranium series dates from Qesem Cave, Israel, and the end of the Lower Palaeolithic". *Nature* 423(6943), 977–979.

Barkai, R., Rosell, J., Blasco, R., & Gopher, A. 2017. "Fire for a reason: barbecue at middle Pleistocene Qesem Cave, Israel". *Current Anthropology* 58(S16), S314–S328.

Ben-Dor, M., Gopher, A., Hershkovitz, I., & Barkai, R. "Man the fat hunter: the demise of Homo erectus and the emergence of a new hominin lineage in the Middle Pleistocene (ca. 400 kyr) Levant". *PLoS One* 6(12), e28689.

Blasco, R., Rosell, J., Sánchez-Marco, A., Gopher, A., & Barkai, R. 2019. "Feathers and food: human–bird interactions at Middle Pleistocene Qesem Cave, Israel". *Human Evolution* 136, 1–17.

Frumkin, A., Karkanas, P., Bar-Matthews, M., Barkai, R., Gopher, A., Shahack-Gross, R., & Vaks, A. 2009. "Gravitational deformations and fillings of aging caves: the example of Qesem karst system, Israel". *Geomorphology* 106(1–2), 154–164.

Halfon, E., & Barkai, R. 2020. "The material and mental effects of animal disappearance on indigenous hunter-gatherers, past and present". *Time and Mind* 13(1), 5–33.

Hershkovitz, I., Smith, P., Sarig, R., Quam, R., Rodríguez, L., García, R., & Gopher, A. 2011. "Middle Pleistocene dental remains from Qesem Cave (Israel)". *American Journal of Physical Anthropology* 144(4), 575–592.

Chapter 5
Books

Churchill, S. E. 2014. *Thin on the Ground: Neandertal Biology, Archeology, and Ecology.* John Wiley & Sons. Hoboken (NJ).

Fagan, B. 2011. *Cro-Magnon: How the Ice Age Gave Birth to the First Modern Humans.* Bloomsbury. New York.

Finlayson, C. 2009. *The Humans Who Went Extinct: Why Neanderthals Died Out and We Survived.* Oxford University Press. Oxford.

Finlayson, C. 2019. *The Smart Neanderthal: Bird-Catching, Cave Art and the Cognitive Revolution.* Oxford University Press. Oxford.

Pääbo, S. 2014. *Neanderthal Man: In Search of Lost Genomes.* Hachette. London.

Spikins, P. 2015. *How Compassion Made Us Human: The Evolutionary Origins of Tenderness, Trust and Morality.* Pen and Sword. Barnsley.

Tattersall, I. 1999. *The Last Neanderthal: The Rise, Success, and Mysterious Extinction of Our Closest Human Relatives.* Westview Press. Boulder (CO).

Papers

Bar-Yosef, O. 2013. "Neanderthals and modern humans across Eurasia". In: Akazawa, T., Nishiaki. Y., and Aoki, K. (eds.). *Dynamics of Learning in Neanderthals and Modern Humans* 1. Springer. Tokyo, 7–20.

Callander, J. 2004. "Dorothy Garrod's excavations in the Late Mousterian of Shukbah Cave in Palestine reconsidered". *Proceedings of the Prehistoric Society* 70, 207–231.

Hawks, J. 2017. "Neanderthals and Denisovans as biological invaders". *Proceedings of the National Academy of Sciences* 114(37), 9761–9763.

Jaubert J., Verheyden S., Genty D., Soulier M., Cheng H., Blamart D., et al. 2016. "Early Neanderthal constructions deep in Bruniquel Cave in southwestern France". *Nature* 534, 111–114.

Lalueza-Fox, C., Rosas, A., & de la Rasilla, M. 2012. "Palaeogenetic research at the El Sidrón Neanderthal site". *Annals of Anatomy (Anatomischer Anzeiger)* 194(1), 133–137.

Panarello, A., Palombo, M. R., Biddittu, I., Di Vito, M. A., Farinaro, G., & Mietto, P. 2020. "On the devil's tracks: unexpected news from the Foresta ichnosite (Roccamonfina volcano, central Italy)". *Quaternary Science*, 35(3), 444–456.

Rogers, A. R., Bohlender, R. J., & Huff, C. D. 2017. "Early history of Neanderthals and Denisovans". *Proceedings of the National Academy of Sciences* 114(37), 9859–9863.

Rosas, A., Martinez-Maza, C., Bastir, M., Garcia-Tabernero, A., Lalueza-Fox, C., Huguet, R., Ortiz, J. E., Julia, R., Soler, V., De Torres, T., Martinez, E., Canaveras, J. C., Sanchez-Moral,

S., Cuezva, S., Lario, J., Santamaria, D., de la Rasilla, M., & Fortea, J. 2006. "Paleobiology and comparative morphology of a late Neandertal sample from El Sidrón, Asturias, Spain". *Proceedings of the National Academy of Sciences* 103(51), 19266–19271

Shea, J. J. 2003. "Neandertals, competition, and the origns of modern human behavior in the Levant." *Evolutionary Anthropology* 12, 173–187.

Smith, P. J., Callander, J., Bahn, P. G., & Pinçon, G. 1997. "Dorothy Garrod in words and pictures." *Antiquity* 71(272), 265.

Speth, J. D. 2012. "Middle Palaeolithic subsistence in the Near East". *Before Farming* 2012(2), 1–45.

Spikins, P., Needham, A., Wright, B., Dytham, C., Gatta, M., & Hitchens, G. 2019. "Living to fight another day: the ecological and evolutionary significance of Neanderthal healthcare". *Quaternary Science Reviews* 217, 98–118.

Chapter 6
Books

Clottes, J. 2003. *Chauvet Cave: The Art of Earliest Times.* University of Utah Press, Salt Lake City.

Clottes, J. 2016. *What is Paleolithic Art? Cave Paintings and the Dawn of Human Creativity.* University of Chicago Press. Chicago.

Clottes, J., & Lewis-Williams, J. D. 1998. *The Shamans of Prehistory: Trance and Magic in the Painted Caves.* Harry N. Abrams. New York.

Coolidge, F. L., & Wynn, T. G. 2018. *The Rise of Homo Sapiens: The Evolution of Modern Thinking.* Oxford University Press. Oxford.

Lewis-Williams, J. D. 2002. *The Mind in the Cave.* Thames & Hudson. London.

Papers

Belfer-Cohen, A., & Goring-Morris, N. 2014. "The Upper Palaeolithic and Earlier Epi-palaeolithic of Western Asia".

In: Renfrew, C., & Bahn, P. (eds.). *The Cambridge World Prehistory*, 1381–1407.

Carbonell, E., & Mosquera, M. 2006. "The emergence of a symbolic behaviour: the sepulchral pit of Sima de los Huesos, Sierra de Atapuerca, Burgos, Spain". *Comptes Rendus Palevol* 5(1–2), 155–160.

Clark, J. D., Beyene, Y., Wolde Gabriel, G., Hart, W. K., Renne, P. R., Gilbert, H., & White, T. D. 2003. "Stratigraphic, chronological and behavioural contexts of Pleistocene Homo sapiens from Middle Awash, Ethiopia". *Nature* 423(6941), 747–752.

Dirks, P. H., Roberts, E. M., Hilbert-Wolf, H., Kramers, J. D., Hawks, J., Dosseto, A., & Berger, L. R. 2017. "The age of Homo naledi and associated sediments in the Rising Star Cave, South Africa". *Elife* 6, e24231.

Harvati, K., Röding, C., Bosman, A. M., Karakostis, F. A., Grün, R., Stringer, C., & Kouloukoussa, M. 2019. "Apidima Cave fossils provide earliest evidence of Homo sapiens in Eurasia". *Nature* 571(7766), 500–504.

Hershkovitz, I., Marder, O., Ayalon, A., Bar-Matthews, M., Yasur, G., Boaretto, E., & Barzilai, O. 2015. "Levantine cranium from Manot Cave (Israel) foreshadows the first European modern humans". *Nature* 520(7546), 216–219.

Hershkovitz, I., Weber, G. W., Quam, R., Duval, M., Grün, R., Kinsley, L., & Weinstein-Evron, M. 2018. "The earliest modern humans outside Africa". *Science* 359(6374), 456–459.

Hublin, J. J., Ben-Ncer, A., Bailey, S. E., Freidline, S. E., Neubauer, S., Skinner, M. M., & Gunz, P. 2017. "New fossils from Jebel Irhoud, Morocco and the pan-African origin of Homo sapiens". *Nature* 546(7657), 289–292.

Kedar, Y., Kedar, G., & Barkai, R. (2021). "Hypoxia in Paleolithic decorated caves: the use of artificial light in deep caves reduces oxygen concentration and induces altered states of consciousness". *Time and Mind* 14(2), 181–216.

White, T. D., Asfaw, B., DeGusta, D., Gilbert, H., Richards, G. D., Suwa, G., & Howell, F. C. 2003. "Pleistocene homo sapiens from middle Awash, Ethiopia". *Nature* 423(6941), 742–747.

Chapter 7
Books
Bar-Yosef, O., & Valla, F. R. (eds.). 2013. *Natufian Culture in the Levant 2*. International Monographs in Prehistory. Ann Arbor (MI) and Belford.

Castaneda, C. 1968. *The Teachings of Don Juan: A Yaqui Way of Knowledge*. University of California Press. Oakland (CA).

Huxley, A. 1954. *The Doors of Perception: And Heaven and Hell*. Harper & Brothers. New York.

Pollan, M. 2018. *How to Change Your Mind: What the New Science of Psychedelics Teaches Us About Consciousness, Dying, Addiction, Depression, and Transcendence*. Michael Pollan. San Francisco.

Shanon, B. 2002. *The Antipodes of the Mind: Charting the Phenomenology of the Ayahuasca Experience*. Oxford University Press. Oxford and New York.

Papers
Bar-Yosef, O. 1998. "The Natufian culture in the Levant: threshold to the origins of agriculture". *Evolutionary Anthropology* 6, 159–177.

Bar-Yosef, O. 2014. "The origins of sedentism and agriculture in Western Asia". In: Renfrew, C., & Bahn, P. (eds.). *The Cambridge World Prehistory*. 1408–1438.

Goldgeier, H., Munro, N. D., & Grosman, L. 2019. "Remembering a sacred place: the depositional history of Hilazon Tachtit, a Natufian burial cave". *Anthropological Archaeology* 56, 101–111.

Grosman, L., & Munro, N. D. 2016. "A Natufian ritual event". *Current Anthropology* 57(3), 311–331.

Grosman, L., Munro, N. D., & Belfer-Cohen, A. 2008. "A 12,000-year-old shaman burial from the southern Levant

(Israel)". *Proceedings of the National Academy of Sciences* 105(46), 17665–17669.

Chapter 8
Books

Barker, G. 2006. *The Agricultural Revolution in Prehistory: Why Did Foragers Become Farmers?*. Oxford University Press. Oxford.

Bellwood, P., Gamble, C., Le Blanc, S. A., Pluciennik, M., Richards, M., & Terrell, J. E. 2005. *First Farmers: The Origins of Agricultural Societies*. Cambridge University Press. Cambridge.

Bocquet-Appel, J.-P., & Bar-Yosef, O. 2008. *The Neolithic Demographic Transition and its Consequences*. Springer. New York.

Cohen M. N. 1977. *The Food Crisis in Prehistory: Overpopulation and the Origins of Agriculture*. Yale University Press. New Haven (CT).

Hodder, I. 2012. *Entangled: An Archaeology of the Relationships between Humans and Things*. Wiley-Blackwell. Oxford.

Hodder, I. 2018. *Where Are We Heading? The Evolution of Humans and Things*. Yale University Press. New Haven (CT).

Kenyon, K. M. 1958. *Digging Up Jericho*. Ernest Benn. London.

Rindos, D. 1984. *The Origins of Agriculture: An Evolutionary Perspective*. Academic Press. New York.

Schmidt, K., & Wittwar, M. 2012. *Göbekli Tepe: A Stone Age Sanctuary in South-Eastern Anatolia*. Ex Oriente e.V. Berlin.

Papers

Abbo, S., & Gopher, A. 2020. "Plant domestication in the Neolithic Near East: the humans–plants liaison." *Quaternary Science Reviews* 242, 106–112.

Bar-Yosef, O. 1995." Earliest food producers – Pre Pottery Neolithic". In: Levy, T. (ed.). *The Archeology of Society in the Holy Land*. 190–204.

Barkai, R., & Liran, R. 2008. "Midsummer sunset at Neolithic Jericho". *Time and Mind: The Journal of Archaeology, Consciousness and Culture* 1(3), 273–284.

Belter-Cohen, A., & Goring-Morris, A. N. 2011. "Becoming Farmers". *Current Anthropology* 52(S4), S209–S220.

Braidwood, R. J. 1960. "The Agricultural Revolution". *Scientific American* 203, 131–148.

Goring-Morris, A. N., & Belfer-Cohen, A. 2011. "Neolithization processes in the Levant". *Current Anthropology* 52(S4), S195–S208.

Liran, R., & Barkai, R. 2011. "Casting a shadow on Neolithic Jericho". *Antiquity* 85(327).

Schmidt, K. 2010. "Göbekli Tepe – the Stone Age sanctuaries: new results of ongoing excavations with a special focus on sculptures and high reliefs". *Documenta Praehistorica* 37, 239–256.

Watkins, T. 1990. "The origins of house and home". *World Archaeology* 21(3), 336–347.

Zeder, M. A. 2008. "Domestication and early agriculture in the Mediterranean Basin: origins, diffusion, and impact". *Proceedings of the National Academy of Sciences* 105(33), 11597–11604.

Chapter 9
Books

Ben-Yosef, E. 2018. *Mining for Ancient Copper: Essays in Memory of Beno Rothenberg*. Eisenbrauns: Penn State University Press. University Park (PA).

Craddock, P. T. 1995. *Early Metal Mining and Production*. Edinburgh University Press, Edinburgh.

Roberts, B. W., & Thornton, C. P. (eds.). 2014. *Archeometallurgy in Global Perspective*. Springer. New York.

Rothenberg, B. 1972. *Timna: Valley of the Biblical Copper Mines*. Thames & Hudson. London.

Shalem, D., Gal, Z., & Smithline, H. 2013. *Peqi'in: A Late Chalcolithic Burial Site Upper Galilee, Israel.* Ostracon. Thessaloniki.

Tylecote, R. F. 1992. *A History of Metallurgy*, 2nd ed. Institute of Materials, Minerals and Mining. London.

Papers

Ben-Yosef, E. 2016. "Back to Solomon's era: results of the first excavations at 'Slaves' Hill' (site 34, Timna, Israel)". *Bulletin of the American Schools of Oriental Research* 376(1), 169–198.

Ben-Yosef, E., Langgut, D., & Sapir-Hen, L. 2017. "Beyond smelting: new insights on Iron Age (10th c. BCE) metalworkers' community from excavations at a gatehouse and associated livestock pens in Timna, Israel". *Journal of Archaeological Science: Reports* 11, 411–426.

Gilead, I., & Gošić, M. 2014. "Fifty years later: a critical review of the stratigraphy, chronology and context of the Nahal Mishmar hoard". *Journal of the Israel Prehistoric Society* 44, 226–239.

Golden, J. 2009. "New light on the development of Chalcolithic metal technology in the Southern Levant". *World Prehistory* 22(3), 283–300.

Goren, Y. 2008. "The location of specialized copper production by the lost wax technique in the Chalcolithic southern Levant". *Geoarchaeology: An International Journal* 23(3), 374–397.

Harney, E., May, H., Shalem, D., Rohland, N., Mallick, S., Lazaridis, I., Sarig, R., Stewardson, K., Nordenfelt, S., Patterson, N., Hershkovitz, I., & Reich, D. 2018. "Ancient DNA from Chalcolithic Israel reveals the role of population mixture in cultural transformation". *Nature Communications* 9, 3336.

Shalem, D. 2015. "Motifs on the Nahal Mishmar hoard and the ossuaries: comparative observations and interpretations". *Journal of the Israel Prehistoric Society* 45, 217–237.

Shalem, D. 2017. "Cultural continuity and changes in South Levantine late Chalcolithic burial customs and iconographic imagery: an interpretation of the finds from the Peqi'in Cave." *Journal of the Israel Prehistoric Society* 47, 148–170.

Shalev, S. 1996. "The Nahal Mishmar hoard and Chalcolithic metallurgy in Israel". *Eres Israel* 25, 274–285.

Tadmor, M., Kedem, D., Begemann, F., Hauptmann, A., & Pernicka, E. 1995. "The Nahal Mishmar hoard from the Judean Desert: technology, composition, and provenance". *Atiqot* 27, 95–148.

Ussishkin, D. 1971. "The 'Ghassulian' temple in Ein Gedi and the origin of the hoard from Nahal Mishmar". *Biblical Archaeologist* 34(1), 23–39.

Chapter 10
Books

Aveni, A. F. 1993. *Ancient Astronomers*. St. Remy Press. Montreal.

Aveni, A. F. 2008. *People and the Sky: Our Ancestors and the Cosmos*. Thames & Hudson. London.

O'Kelly, M. J., & O'Kelly, C. 1982. *Newgrange: Archaeology, Art and Legend*. Thames & Hudson. London.

Parker Pearson, M. 2012. *Stonehenge: Exploring the Greatest Stone Age Mystery*. Simon and Schuster. London.

Parker Pearson, M., Pollard, J., Richards, C., Thomas, J., & Welham, K. 2015. *Stonehenge: Making Sense of a Prehistoric Mystery*. Council for British Archaeology. York.

Ruggles, C. 1999. *Astronomy in Prehistoric Britain and Ireland*. Yale University Press. New Haven (CT).

Ruggles, C. 2005. *Ancient Astronomy: An Encyclopedia of Cosmologies and Myth*. ABC-CLIO. Santa Barbara (CA).

Ruggles, C. L. (ed.). *Handbook of Archeoastronomy and Ethnoastronomy*. Springer. New York.

Papers

Arav, R. 2011. "Excarnation: food for vultures. Unlocking the mysteries of Chalcolithic ossuaries". *Biblical Archaeology Review* 37(6), 40–47.

Aveni, A., & Mizrachi, Y. 1998. "The geometry and astronomy of Rujm el-Hiri, a megalithic site in the southern Levant". *Field Archaeology* 25(4), 475–496.

Freikman, M. 2016. "The Chalcolithic settlement of el-Arbain: reassessing the Chalcolithic culture of the Golan". *Journal of the Israel Prehistoric Society* 46, 20–67.

Freikman, M. 2017. "Into the darkness: deep caves in the ancient Near East". *Landscape Ecology* 10(3), 81–99.

Freikman, M., & Porat, N. 2017. "Rujm el-Hiri: the monument in the landscape." *Tel Aviv* 44(1), 14–39.

Ilan, D., & Rowan, Y. 2019. "Expediting reincarnation in the fifth millennium BCE: interpreting the Chalcolithic ossuaries of the southern Levant". *Oxford Journal of Archaeology* 38(3), 248–270.

Zohar, M. 1989. "Rogem Hiri: a megalithic monument in the Golan". *Israel Exploration Journal* 39(1–2), 18–31.

Books That Inspired Us

Brown, T. 1986. *The Tracker*. Berkley Books. New York.

Chatwin, B. 1987. *The Songlines*. Penguin Books. London.

De Wall, F. 1996. *Good Natured: The Origins of Right and Wrong in Humans and Other Animals*. Harvard University Press. Cambridge (MA).

De Wall, F. 2005. *Our Inner Ape*. Riverhead Books. New York

De Wall, F. 2016. *Are We Smart Enough to Know How Smart Animals Are?* Granta Books. London.

Diamond, J. 1992. *The Third Chimpanzee: The Evolution and Future of the Human Animal*. Hutchinson Radius. London.

Diamond, J. 1997. *Guns, Germs, and Steel: The Fates of Human Societies*. Norton Books. New York.

Diamond, J. 2005. *Collapse: How Societies Choose to Fail or Succeed*. Viking Penguin. New York.

Goodall, J. 1971. *In the Shadow of Man*. Houghton Mifflin Harcourt. Boston (MA).

Lévi-Strauss, C. 1966. *The Savage Mind*. University of Chicago Press. Chicago.

Montagu, A. 1976. *The Nature of Human Aggression.* Oxford University Press. Oxford.

Pepperberg, I. 2009. *Alex and Me: How a Scientist and a Parrot Discovered a Hidden World of Animal Intelligence and Formed a Deep Bond in the Process.* Harper Perennial. New York.

Quinn, D. 1992. *Ishmael.* Bantam Books. New York.

Quinn, D. 1996. *The Story of B.* Bantam Books. New York.

Syomushkin, T. 1952. *Alitet Goes to the Hills.* Foreign Languages Publishing House. Moscow.

Verne, J. 1999. *The Eternal Adam.* Phoenix. London.

Winston, R. 2002. *The Human Instinct: How Our Primeval Impulses Shape Our Modern Lives.* Transworld Publishers. London.

Relevant Inspiring Books for Children and Young People

Beauclerk Maurice, E. 2004. *The Last of the Gentlemen Adventurers: Coming of Age in the Arctic.* 4th Estate. London.

de Fombell, T. 2009. *Toby Alone.* Walker Book. London.

de Fombell, T. 2010. *Toby and the Secrets of the Tree.* Walker Books. London.

Paver, M. 2004. *Brother Wolf.* Katherine Tegen Books. New York.

Paver, M. 2005. *Spirit Walker.* Katherine Tegen Books. New York.

Paver, M. 2006. *Soul Eater.* Katherine Tegen Books. New York.

ACKNOWLEDGMENTS

This book was written on the basis of many dozens of books and hundreds of articles. Behind each of these works are world-class scientists, scholars, and researchers, in a range of fields and subjects. Some of them were mentioned and quoted in the course of the book, and others appear in the abridged list of further reading at the end, but there were many others who accompanied us even before we started this journey and this work. We thank them for enriching our knowledge and our world, and for being by our side even without knowing it. The readiness and helpfulness of everyone we asked for a field tour or a meeting, or at least an informal chat about their areas of expertise, cannot be taken for granted—especially in this competitive, frenetic, and busy academic environment. Here we wish to thank Adrian Tanner, Miki Ben-Dor, Daniella Bar Yosef-Mayer, Leore Grosman, Dina Shalem, Kathryn Arthur, Lisa Lucero, Meir Finkel, Michael Freikman, Yoni Mizrahi, Micha Ankori, Yorke Rowan, Trevor Watkins, Dandan Bolotin, Izzy Marimski, Naama Goren-Inbar, Erez Ben-Yosef, and Nurith Goshen. A special thanks to the late Ofer Bar- Yosef, who managed to share some of his insights and memories with us a few weeks before his death.

We have reprinted the pictures in this book with the generous help and permission of many of those in the above list, and in addition to them, we were also aided by Ofer Marder, Dov Ganchrow, David Lordkipanidze, Nino Grigolava, Frédéric Plassard, Jean Clottes, Ruth Blasco, Jordi Rosell, Jordi Serangeli, and Nicholas Conrad.

Members of the prehistoric archeology lab at Tel Aviv University took an active part in conversations and deliberations: reading some of the chapters, joining some of our excursions, and even conducting some of the studies mentioned in this book.

Thank to Shmuel Rosner and Yael Neemani, our editors at Kinneret-Zemora- Dvir publishers.

We really hope that this book would reach readers for whom Hebrew is not their language and Israel is not their home. To a certain extent we wrote it for them. If you have come this far, it is thanks to Watkins Publishing, who located *They Were Here Before Us* and found it worthy. We were lucky to work with Eyalon Levy, who translated the text with talent and dedication; Fiona Robertson, a publisher who was attentive to all our requests and knew how to mediate between our Mediterranean temperament and what is acceptable in the United Kingdom; and Ingrid Court-Jones, who meticulously edited the final version that is placed before you. Special thanks to foreign rights agent Ziv Lewish, and our friend and lawyer Michel Kains for all their legal effort.

Both of us are extremely obsessive about what we do and focused on ourselves and what interests us. Thanks to our families, for keeping us anchored in the real world.

Ran Barkai and Eyal Halfon

INDEX